SIMPLY GOOD FOOD
NEIL PERRY

SIMPLY GOOD FOOD
NEIL PERRY

PHOTOGRAPHY BY EARL CARTER
STYLING BY SUE FAIRLIE-CUNINGHAME

MURDOCH BOOKS

ACKNOWLEDGEMENTS

This book brought the team back together in the studio and also brought a new publishing and design team to the task. For their efforts I would like to thank:

The great team cooking my food: Sarah Swan – old hand, she still has it – and Mike Clift – fabulous young cook who is joining the Rockpool Qantas Consulting team. Nice work.

Stephanie Young, my PA, for all the effort getting me in the right place at the right time.

Sue Hines, Publishing Director. I did my very first book with you in the '90s – good to give it another go twenty years later.

Diana Hill – your patience and calm disposition got the best out of us.

Claire Grady – nice bit of project management, we did set a crazy deadline.

Hugh Ford – nice clean design and thanks for making the book I imagined.

Earl Carter and Sue Fairlie-Cuninghame – what can I say? Your creative insight make me look good and as always, I'm so pleased with your work, as well as your friendship. Big kisses.

And the biggest kisses of all to my chicks Samantha, Josephine, Macy and Indy. You make my life full of beautiful women... wonderful.

This book is dedicated to my dear friend and mentor David Coe.
Coey, as he was known, lived a full and rich life in his all too short 58 years.
He left behind an amazing wife and three sons and a group of friends whose
lives were better for having known him – in many cases he was the force
that brought them together. He was certainly one of the best people on this
planet and the memory of him will be with me forever. I'm a much better
person for having known him.

CONTENTS

The recipes begin on **page 12** with a few of my favourite **cocktails**, followed on **page 16** by simple **soups and salads** which work beautifully as either the perfect start to a meal or a wonderful lunch. A few simple **pasta** dishes follow on **page 42** – all that's required to serve is a dusting of cheese and a good glass of wine. From **page 55** you'll find the **chicken** dishes, from spicy to roast and lots of great flavours in between (the Caramel chicken wings are a real family favourite). From **page 68 pork** is the protein of choice, followed by **beef**, **veal** and **lamb** recipes. My **Asian banquets** start on **page 100**, followed by the **Mediterranean shared tables** on **page 136**. Recipes for **Mexican feasts**, found from **page 172**, are dishes crying out for their place on a table, paired with shaved cabbage and wrapped in tortillas. The **sweet things** begin on **page 190**. All these recipes are delicious and the results are well worth the effort. Happy cooking and enjoy.

My sentiment for this book is the same as for *Easy Weekends* and the inspiration for these recipes comes largely from my column in the *Good Weekend*. My hope is that having simple, produce-driven recipes at your fingertips will inspire you to cook more at home for friends and loved ones.

It is based on the same philosophy: eating healthy, fresh food and buying well will deliver a healthy lifestyle. Buy quality and eat in season, eat in moderation and spoil yourself occasionally, add some light exercise and moderation in drinking and what more could you want in life?

This book is again an expression of my love of multicultural cooking. I not only enjoy eating in the diverse ethnic landscape that is Sydney, but I love being inspired by those trips to little restaurants in my own kitchen at home. My love of all these different cuisines comes to life in this book. It is a measure of how interesting eating can be in this amazing country, built out of immigration and with fabulous produce.

As I was compiling the recipes for *Simply Good Food* I noticed there were a number of really yummy Mexican dishes that would work well together, and for that matter many Asian-inspired and Mediterranean dishes as well. I have grouped these, so if you want you can cook some lovely banquets, or just cook the single dish – it's entirely up to you.

I shouldn't have to say it as I have been banging on about it for years, but please think about what you buy and look to animals that have been humanely raised and looked after. Yes, we eat them, but it doesn't have to be a horror for them from start to finish. Buy Australian seafood – that way you will be sure where it came from – and although we are still working through what sustainable fishing means, we are way ahead of many of the other places we import from. I know we all have budgets, so try to buy the best you can afford and look at how eating simply one day can have you feasting the next while sticking to a budget.

Eat in season. It's cheaper, tastier and much more fun waiting for the first asparagus or raspberries to arrive on the market than it is eating Peruvian or American ones out of season. It doesn't make sense – not just because of the lack of flavour but also because of the carbon footprint.

Again I'd like to stress that this book is about simple and tasty cooking – you don't have to be an amazing chef to get great results. If you are learning to cook, start with the simpler recipes with fewer ingredients and as you grow in confidence add more and more recipes to your repertoire. Cooking is a learned skill not a natural gift, so persistence pays off.

Enjoy these recipes and I hope they make you and your friends and family happy as you sit around a table and enjoy your efforts. Cooking good food for family and friends is a labour of love and there are few things more rewarding for you – the cook and carer.

Most of all have fun with this. Remember, a happy cook makes happy food, which means lots of memories for a life well lived through food, drink and love.

Neil Perry x

AMERICANO

SERVES 1

30 ml (1 fl oz) Campari
30 ml (1 fl oz) sweet vermouth
soda water
1 slice of orange, to garnish

Pour the Campari and vermouth into a tall glass filled with ice. Top with the soda water and garnish with the orange slice and a stirrer.

You will need a cocktail shaker for this classic shaken margarita. There are any number of glasses you can use – just pick something that suits your style.

MARGARITA

SERVES 1

1 lime wedge, to salt the glass
sea salt for the glass, crushed till fine
50 ml (1¾ fl oz) tequila (I like Calle 23 Blanco)
30 ml (1 fl oz) fresh lime juice
20 ml (½ fl oz/1 tablespoon) Cointreau

Salt the rim of the glass by running the edge of a lime wedge around it, then dipping it into the salt – I find the best way is to lay a shallow layer of salt in a saucer. You can of course also use table salt if you prefer. Pour the tequila, lime juice and Cointreau into a cocktail shaker with a handful of ice and give it a good shake. Strain into a coupe glass. This can also be served over ice, the choice is yours.

ITALIAN SOUR NO. 3

30 ml (1 fl oz) Aperol

10 ml (2 teaspoons) Strega (an Italian liqueur)

5 ml (1 teaspoon) Campari

20 ml (½ fl oz/1 tablespoon) fresh pink grapefruit juice

20 ml (½ fl oz/1 tablespoon) fresh lemon juice

dash of egg white

a twist of grapefruit zest, to garnish

Add all the ingredients to a cocktail shaker with a small handful of ice and give a good shake. Strain into a wine glass over cubed ice and garnish with the grapefruit twist and a stirrer.

I'm a fan of Hendrick's Gin, but you can use Bombay Sapphire, Tanqueray – whichever suits your palate. We make our own tonic water at Rockpool, but a great option for home is to get yourself a soda syphon, then you can create soda and tonic to your heart's desire.

GIN & HOUSE TONIC

30 ml (1 fl oz) gin

100 ml (3½ fl oz) homemade tonic

lime wedge, to garnish

Simply build this drink in a short glass by pouring the gin over ice and adding tonic to just below the rim. Garnish with the wedge of lime and off you go.

Any green vegetable, such as zucchini, broccoli or spinach, works well in this soup (in place of the asparagus), or try a combination of all three.

CREAM OF ASPARAGUS SOUP WITH PARMESAN CROUTONS

SERVES 4

60 g (2¼ oz) butter
1 tablespoon extra virgin olive oil
1 leek, white part only, trimmed, washed and roughly chopped
3 garlic cloves, finely chopped
sea salt and freshly ground black pepper
650 g (1 lb 7 oz/4 bunches) asparagus, trimmed, cut into 3 cm (1¼ inch) lengths
1 large all-purpose potato (eg desiree), peeled and roughly chopped
800 ml (28 fl oz) chicken stock
150 ml (5 fl oz) thin (pouring) cream
1 tablespoon fresh lemon juice

PARMESAN CROUTONS
80 g (2¾ oz/1 cup) finely diced day-old sourdough bread (or any kind of dense bread)
1 tablespoon olive oil
sea salt and freshly ground white pepper
3 tablespoons freshly grated parmesan cheese

Preheat the oven to 200°C (400°F/Gas 6).

Heat the butter and oil in a large, heavy-based saucepan. Add the leek, garlic, salt and pepper and sweat over low heat until the leek is soft. Add the asparagus and potato and cook over medium heat for 3–4 minutes or until the vegetables are lightly coated in the butter mixture.

Add the stock and simmer over medium heat for 15–20 minutes or until the asparagus and potato are tender. Transfer the mixture to a blender and process until smooth.

Return the mixture to the saucepan, add the cream and lemon juice, and heat until just warmed through. Remove from the heat and season to taste.

For the croutons, combine the bread with the oil, salt and pepper and toss to coat. Place the bread on a baking tray in one layer and bake for 4–6 minutes or until lightly golden.

Remove the croutons from the oven and sprinkle with the parmesan. Bake for another 1–2 minutes or until the croutons are brown and crisp, tossing to prevent them burning. Allow to cool on the tray.

Serve the soup in large bowls topped with a spoonful or two of the croutons.

NOTE: The croutons will keep for a few days in an airtight container in a dry place. They can be tossed through any salad for added crunch, and go especially well in a Caesar.

This dip also works well with Turkish bread or sliced baguette. You can serve it on top of lettuce leaves. I like baby cos or iceberg because of the crunch.

SMOKED OCEAN TROUT DIP WITH LEMON THYME TOAST

SERVES 4

600 g (1 lb 5 oz) hot smoked ocean trout
125 g (4½ oz/½ cup) crème fraîche
2 lemons, zested and juiced
15 g (½ oz/¼ cup) finely chopped dill
sea salt and freshly ground black pepper

LEMON THYME TOAST
150 ml (5 fl oz) extra virgin olive oil
2 garlic cloves
2 tablespoons lemon thyme leaves
3 pieces large pitta bread

Preheat the oven to 180°C (350°F/Gas 4).

For the dip, remove the trout skin and use a fork to roughly flake the flesh. Combine the crème fraîche, lemon zest and juice and dill, and season with salt and pepper. Gently fold through the trout pieces and check the seasoning.

For the toasts, heat the oil, garlic cloves and lemon thyme together in a small saucepan. Once the garlic starts to blister, turn off the heat and set aside. Cool.

Cut the pitta bread into 10–12 pieces, place on a lined baking tray and toast in the oven for a few minutes or until lightly golden. Brush with the lemon thyme oil and serve immediately with the smoked ocean trout dip.

NOTE: The lemon thyme oil can be made a few days ahead of time. It's also great brushed over grilled fish or chicken.

Any seafood can be substituted for the crab in this versatile salad – try cubes of raw fish, marinated for 5 minutes in lime juice, or chunks of hot smoked trout or eel. I also like this salad with pieces of roast chicken or duck instead of the crab. For a wonderful crunch, add croutons. Fry torn stale bread in extra virgin olive oil until golden brown, then toss through the salad.

SPANNER CRAB WITH TOMATO & CUCUMBER SALAD

SERVES 4

80 ml (2½ fl oz/⅓ cup) extra virgin olive oil

2 lemons

sea salt and freshly ground black pepper

1 baby cos (romaine) lettuce, leaves separated and torn

16 cherry tomatoes, halved (see note)

2 Lebanese (short) cucumbers, peeled, halved lengthways, seeded and cut into 1 cm (½ inch) half moons

2 large fresh jalapeño chillies, halved lengthways, seeded and chopped

½ small red onion, finely chopped

2 tablespoons finely chopped flat-leaf (Italian) parsley

500 g (1 lb 2 oz) cooked spanner crab meat, picked over to remove any shell or cartilage

To make the dressing, place the oil, the juice of 2 lemons, the zest of 1 lemon, salt and pepper to taste in a small bowl, and mix well.

In a separate bowl, place the cos leaves and one-third of the dressing, season with pepper, toss gently and divide among four serving plates.

Place the remaining ingredients, except for the crab, in the bowl and dress with half the remaining dressing. Place the salad on top of the leaves (try to keep it together, but don't fret if it slides off).

Place the crab and the last bit of dressing in the bowl and mix to coat the crab. Place a mound of crab on each salad. Finish with a good grind of pepper and a sprinkle of sea salt.

NOTE: Use any beautiful tomatoes you can find – cherry, Kumato or vine-ripened.

Any good-quality fish works well in this recipe and prawn or lobster would be fabulous. If you don't like fish, substitute the same weight of mussels or clams, shell them and then add the salad ingredients. Cooked crab meat or cooked king prawns will also work well. Shredded roast chicken from a good chicken shop turns this into a five-minute meal.

SCALLOP CEVICHE WITH GINGER, CHILLI & CORN

SERVES 4

500 g (1 lb 2 oz) raw scallops
1 tablespoon very finely chopped ginger
½ red onion, finely chopped
juice of 4 limes
3 tablespoons extra virgin olive oil
2 wild green chillies, finely chopped
1 bunch coriander (cilantro), leaves only
1 small orange sweet potato (about
    300 g/10½ oz), peeled, cut into
    5 mm (¼ inch) dice, boiled
    until tender
1 corn cob, kernels only
sea salt and freshly ground black pepper

Place the scallops, ginger, onion and half the lime juice in a bowl and set aside for 5 minutes. Drain off the juices, add all the remaining ingredients to the bowl and season with salt and pepper.

Spoon the ceviche into four beautiful glasses, such as martini glasses, and serve.

Prawns, salmon or ocean trout are good substitutes for the tuna. Chicken, quail or pork also work well – just adjust the cooking times and cook the chicken and pork all the way through. When making the tuna crust, do take the time to toast the spices as it brings out the essential oils and makes a huge difference to the flavour.

SPICE-CRUSTED TUNA, TOMATO & BUTTERBEAN SALAD

SERVES 4

2 teaspoons whole white peppercorns

2 teaspoons fennel seeds

pinch of coriander seeds

1 teaspoon cumin seeds

1 teaspoon sea salt, plus extra, to season

500 g (1 lb 2 oz) sashimi-grade tuna loin, skin and bloodline removed

2 handfuls baby rocket (arugula) leaves

60 g (2¼ oz) butterbeans, diagonally sliced, blanched and refreshed

55 g (2 oz/¼ cup) drained semi-dried (sun-blushed) tomatoes or cherry tomatoes

extra virgin olive oil

freshly ground white pepper

PRESERVED LEMON DRESSING

3 tablespoons extra virgin olive oil

juice of ½ lemon

1 teaspoon finely chopped preserved lemon zest

sea salt and freshly ground black pepper

Toast all the spices in a dry frying pan until fragrant, then remove from the heat and set aside to cool.

Grind the sea salt with the spices in a mortar with a pestle to form a coarse powder. Spread the spice mix over a plate.

Cut the tuna in half lengthways and roll each piece in the spice mixture until evenly coated. Sear the tuna in a well-heated oiled frying pan over high heat until it is cooked 5–6 mm (¼ inch) of the way through on each side. Allow to cool and then wrap and refrigerate until needed.

For the dressing, whisk all the ingredients to combine. Season to taste with salt and pepper.

For the salad, place the rocket leaves, beans and tomatoes in a small bowl. Add enough preserved lemon dressing to just coat. Toss to combine. Taste and adjust the seasoning if necessary.

Arrange the salad on a plate and top with the tuna slices. Drizzle the tuna with a little olive oil and a sprinkling of sea salt and white pepper. Serve immediately.

NOTE: Simply double the quantities and you have a fantastic summer main course salad for lunch or dinner. All that's required is a quality chilled white wine and you're in business. If cutting the beans is too much for you, simply open a tin of cooked white beans such as cannellini and rinse. They have a wonderful affinity with tuna and are great to keep in the cupboard for simple meals when you don't feel like cooking the beans from scratch.

This salad is great as a starter or as part of a shared family table. The leeks could be replaced with fresh asparagus or artichokes, which have either been cooked, or sliced thinly and served raw.

LEEKS & SOFT EGGS WITH GARLIC VINAIGRETTE

SERVES 4

10 garlic cloves
sea salt and freshly ground black pepper
125 ml (4 fl oz/½ cup) extra virgin
    olive oil
1½ tablespoons red wine vinegar
4 eggs, organic, if possible
4 small–medium leeks, white part only,
    trimmed and washed
freshly grated parmesan cheese
½ bunch chives, finely snipped, to serve

Bring a small saucepan of salted water to the boil. Add the garlic, reduce the heat and simmer until very tender. Strain the garlic and mash it in a bowl. Add the salt, pepper, olive oil and vinegar and whisk until incorporated.

Cook the eggs, straight from the fridge, in boiling salted water for 6 minutes. Transfer to a bowl of iced water to cool. Peel the eggs.

In a large saucepan of boiling salted water, gently simmer the leeks for 8–10 minutes or until tender. Drain the leeks on paper towel. Carefully remove the first layer of skin from each leek and cut the leeks in half lengthways then cut each half into lengths approximately 5 cm (2 inches) long. While still warm, dress with the garlic vinaigrette and mix through the parmesan.

Place the leeks on a large serving dish or divide among four plates. Cut the eggs in half and place on the leeks, spoon over any extra dressing and sprinkle with the chives and black pepper.

NOTE: Leeks are a much-underused vegetable. Try them boiled, roasted or grilled on the barbecue.

Prawns are lovely in this salad, either as a substitute for the chicken or added with the chicken. The chicken and dressing are also tasty when served with steamed rice instead of noodles.

CHICKEN & NOODLE SALAD WITH SPICY SESAME DRESSING

SERVES 4, OR 8 AS PART OF A SHARED ASIAN BANQUET

250 ml (9 fl oz/1 cup) Shaoxing rice wine or dry sherry

3 garlic cloves, sliced

8 cm (3¼ inch) piece fresh ginger, peeled and sliced

½ bunch spring onions (scallions), dark green ends only, plus 2 spring onions, extra

250 g (9 oz) skinless chicken breast fillets (free-range or organic, if possible)

6 iceberg lettuce leaves, shredded

150 g (5½ oz) fresh egg noodles, blanched and refreshed, drained

2 tablespoons chopped coriander (cilantro) leaves

SPICY SESAME DRESSING

1 teaspoon finely chopped fresh ginger

1 teaspoon finely chopped garlic

3 tablespoons thick soy sauce

1 teaspoon sugar

2 teaspoons Chinkiang black vinegar

2 teaspoons sesame sauce

1 teaspoon ground chilli powder

2 tablespoons chilli oil (see note)

Place the Shaoxing, garlic, ginger, spring onion ends and 1 litre (35 fl oz/4 cups) water in a saucepan over high heat and bring to the boil. Add the chicken, reduce the heat and simmer for 2 minutes.

Remove the pan from the heat and allow to stand for 20 minutes, then remove the chicken.

Mix all the dressing ingredients until well incorporated.

Shred the chicken by hand. Shred the white and green parts of the remaining 2 spring onions.

Combine the lettuce, noodles and coriander in a bowl with two-thirds of the dressing. Place the noodle mixture in the middle of a large plate. Top with the chicken and pour over the rest of the dressing. Sprinkle the shredded spring onions over the top.

NOTE: It's worth going to the effort of making your own chilli oil. Lightly toast 20 seeded dried long red chillies, then grind them in a spice grinder. Heat 500 ml (17 fl oz/2 cups) of vegetable or peanut oil to 155°C (300°F) and pour it on the chilli powder. Leave for 1 hour, then strain.

MANCHEGO & CORN FRITTERS

75 g (2½ oz/½ cup) plain (all-purpose)
   flour
1 egg whisked with 2 tablespoons milk
60 g (2¼ oz/1 cup) Japanese
   breadcrumbs (panko)
vegetable oil, for deep-frying

CAPSICUM JAM
3 tablespoons extra virgin olive oil
1 brown onion, thinly sliced
3 tablespoons caster (superfine) sugar
1 teaspoon sea salt
3 tablespoons good-quality sherry vinegar
2 large red capsicums (peppers), seeded
   and thinly sliced
sea salt and freshly ground black pepper

BECHAMEL
250 ml (9 fl oz/1 cup) milk
1 fresh bay leaf, gently bruised
½ thyme sprig
1 small garlic clove, crushed with the
   back of a knife
1 whole clove
40 g (1½ oz) unsalted butter
35 g (1¼ oz/¼ cup) plain (all-purpose)
   flour

MANCHEGO AND CORN FRITTERS
25 g (1 oz) unsalted butter
1 brown onion, finely chopped
200 g (7 oz/1 cup) fresh corn kernels
25 g (1 oz/⅓ cup) finely grated
   Manchego cheese
sea salt and freshly ground black pepper

For the jam, heat the oil in a large saucepan over medium heat. Add the onion and stir occasionally for 5 minutes or until soft and just starting to colour. Add the sugar and salt and cook until the onion starts to caramelise. Deglaze with the vinegar, then add the capsicum, stirring frequently, over low heat for 1–1½ hours or until the mixture is jammy in consistency. Check the seasoning and add more salt and pepper if desired. The jam is best served at room temperature but can be made ahead of time and refrigerated.

For the béchamel, combine the milk, herbs, garlic and clove in a saucepan over medium heat and bring to a simmer. Remove from the heat and allow the mixture to stand for 1 hour to let the flavours infuse. Strain into a clean saucepan and warm over low heat.

Melt the butter in a saucepan over medium heat, add the flour and stir constantly for a few minutes or until sandy in colour. Gradually add the warm infused milk, one ladleful at a time, whisking after each addition to incorporate. Then cook, beating vigorously with a wooden spoon, for 3–5 minutes or until thick and smooth. Set aside and keep warm covered with plastic wrap or baking paper to avoid a skin forming on top.

For the fritters, melt the butter in a frying pan over low heat. Cook the onion until soft and translucent. Add the corn and cook for a further 5 minutes or until soft. Process two-thirds of the corn mixture in a food processor until smooth. Transfer to a bowl then fold through the remaining corn mixture, the Manchego and the béchamel. Season to taste. Spread on a tray and refrigerate for 1–2 hours or until firm.

Place the flour, egg mixture and panko crumbs in three separate bowls. Once the fritter mix is firm, roll into egg-sized pieces and flatten slightly. Dip the fritters into the flour, then the egg mix and then the crumbs, shaking off the excess.

Heat the oil in a deep-fryer or deep saucepan to 180°C (350°F) (or until a cube of bread dropped into the oil turns golden brown in 15 seconds). As soon as a fritter is placed in the oil it should start to bubble. Fry the fritters in batches for 2–3 minutes each or until golden and cooked through. Drain well on paper towel. Serve the fritters with the capsicum jam.

Serve with baby spinach or salad leaves dressed in extra virgin olive oil and aged balsamic. Top the frittata with feta cheese for added bite.

GARDEN GREENS FRITTATA

SERVES 4

8 eggs, organic, if possible

5 g (⅛ oz/¼ cup) flat-leaf (Italian) parsley leaves, roughly chopped

1 tablespoon finely chopped chives

sea salt and freshly ground black pepper

3 tablespoons extra virgin olive oil

1 zucchini (courgette), trimmed and thinly sliced lengthways

2 garlic cloves, finely chopped

1 tablespoon rosemary leaves, finely chopped

1 tablespoon thyme leaves, finely chopped

3 large silverbeet (Swiss chard) leaves, washed and roughly chopped

finely grated pecorino cheese and crisp bacon slices (optional), to serve

Preheat the oven to 180°C (350°F/Gas 4).

In a bowl, whisk the eggs, parsley and chives. Season with salt and pepper to taste.

Heat 1 tablespoon of the oil in a 20 cm (8 inch) non-stick ovenproof frying pan over medium–high heat. Cook the zucchini until lightly golden on both sides. Drain on paper towel.

In the same pan over medium heat, add 1 tablespoon of the oil and sauté the garlic, rosemary and thyme until fragrant and the garlic is soft. Add the silverbeet and cook for 1 minute or until the greens start to wilt. Remove from the heat and transfer the mixture to a bowl.

Heat the remaining oil in the same frying pan over medium heat. Add the egg mixture and cook, without stirring, until the outside begins to set. Use a spatula to start stirring the eggs, lifting up the set egg so the uncooked egg runs underneath. Continue to cook for a further 1 minute, then spoon the silverbeet mixture and the grilled zucchini over the eggs, pressing down gently and spooning some of the raw egg over the top so the vegetables are covered.

Sprinkle with salt and pepper then transfer the pan to the oven. Cook the frittata for 10–15 minutes or until the egg is golden on top and just set.

Serve sprinkled with pecorino and with bacon on the side, if desired.

This dish is hot! I love hot bean paste and the dressing also has chilli powder. Both will give a different type of heat and both add nice complexity. If you want to wimp out, remove the chilli powder not the bean paste.

SPICY OCTOPUS SALAD

SERVES 4, OR 8 AS PART OF A SHARED ASIAN BANQUET

½ celery heart, finely chopped
1 spring onion (scallion), julienned
1 small carrot, julienned
½ small Lebanese (short) cucumber, halved lengthways, seeded and julienned
¼ small daikon radish, julienned
¼ small Chinese cabbage (wong bok), finely shredded
sea salt
400 g (14 oz) cleaned baby octopus
1 tablespoon vegetable oil
2 teaspoons sesame seeds, roasted

DRESSING
2 tablespoons finely chopped fresh ginger
2 tablespoons finely chopped garlic
3 tablespoons hot bean paste
freshly ground black pepper
2 teaspoons ground chilli powder
1 tablespoon sesame oil
4 tablespoons caster (superfine) sugar
2 teaspoons sea salt

Mix all the dressing ingredients in a bowl with 1 tablespoon water and allow the flavour to develop.

Place the celery, spring onion, carrot, cucumber, radish and cabbage in a bowl and sprinkle generously with sea salt. Toss together and leave for 10 minutes, then rinse under cold water and squeeze dry.

Toss the octopus with the oil and season with a little sea salt, then barbecue over high heat until just cooked through. Set aside to cool slightly and halve if large.

To serve, mix together the vegetables, the warm octopus and the dressing and sprinkle with the sesame seeds.

NOTE: Blanched squid or cooked king prawns are a good substitute for the octopus.

Instead of using cooked prawns, you can marinate raw ones in the lime juice for 3 minutes. This gives the prawns an interesting texture and is probably my favourite way to eat prawns.

KING PRAWN & GREEN PAPAYA SALAD WITH NAM JIM DRESSING

SERVES 4, OR 8 AS PART OF A SHARED ASIAN BANQUET

12 large cooked king prawns (shrimp), peeled, deveined and tails intact

½ small green papaya, seeded and skin removed, julienned

2 small Lebanese (short) cucumbers, halved lengthways, seeded and thinly sliced on the angle into half moons

250 g (9 oz) cherry tomatoes, halved

1 small French shallot (eschalot), peeled and thinly sliced

1 small handful coriander (cilantro) leaves

1 small handful Thai basil leaves

1 small handful mint leaves, roughly torn

1 small handful Vietnamese mint leaves, roughly torn

NAM JIM DRESSING

3 garlic cloves, finely chopped

4 coriander (cilantro) roots, finely chopped

½ teaspoon sea salt

2 tablespoons light palm sugar (jaggery), crumbled

2 tablespoons fish sauce

½ fresh long red chilli, seeded and finely chopped

½ fresh long green chilli, seeded and finely chopped

juice of 2 large limes

For the dressing, pound the garlic, coriander roots and sea salt in a mortar with a pestle until a rough paste forms. Remove and place in a bowl.

Dissolve the palm sugar in the fish sauce in a mortar, ensuring there are no lumps of sugar. Add the garlic and coriander mix, along with the red and green chillies and stir well to combine. Add the lime juice. Taste and adjust if necessary to ensure there is a balance of sweet, sour and salty.

Mix all the salad ingredients together in a large bowl and add enough dressing to wet the salad. Mix through thoroughly. Share between four plates and top with any leftover dressing. Serve immediately.

NOTE: Any seafood, or a combination of a few types such as prawns and scallops, works well in this salad. To give the dressing its sourness and a different flavour you can use tamarind instead of lime juice or a combination of tamarind and lime juice.

Any tinned pulses taste a treat here, particularly chickpeas, lentils and white beans. Serve with rice pilaf or steamed rice for a fantastic combination.

LENTILS WITH TAMARIND SAUCE

SERVES 6–8

125 ml (4 fl oz/½ cup) light vegetable oil
1 cup thinly sliced red onion
2 teaspoons finely chopped garlic
1 teaspoon ground turmeric
1 teaspoon smoked paprika
250 g (9 oz) tinned chopped tomatoes
1 tablespoon grated fresh ginger
250 ml (9 fl oz/1 cup) tamarind water
    (see note)
2 x 400 g (14 oz) tinned lentils, drained
    and liquid reserved
1½ teaspoons garam masala
1 teaspoon ground roasted cumin
sea salt and freshly ground black pepper
4 red Asian shallots, thinly sliced

Heat the oil in a large heavy-based frying pan over medium heat. Add the onion and fry until lightly browned, stirring so it doesn't stick and burn. Add the garlic and cook for a further 2 minutes. Add the turmeric and paprika and cook for 1 minute. Add the tomatoes and ginger and cook for a further 5 minutes.

Add the tamarind water and the reserved lentil liquid. Simmer the mixture, covered, over low heat for 15–20 minutes.

Add the lentils, garam masala and cumin and cook for 3 minutes or until the lentils are heated through. Check seasoning, place in a bowl and sprinkle with the shallots.

NOTE: Tamarind can be bought either in water form ready to go, or as a pulp where you soak it in hot water then strain.

The horseradish mayonnaise can be served as a dipping sauce with roasted potatoes or vegetables or spread onto a steak sandwich or burger.

ROAST BEEF GORGONZOLA WITH HORSERADISH POTATO SALAD

SERVES 4

40 g (1½ oz) hazelnuts
olive oil, for frying
400 g (14 oz) beef fillet
sea salt and freshly ground black pepper
½ bunch watercress, picked, washed and dried
120 g (4¼ oz) gorgonzola cheese, crumbled

HORSERADISH MAYONNAISE
120 g (4¼ oz/½ cup) whole-egg mayonnaise
2 tablespoons good-quality creamed horseradish
1 small garlic clove, finely chopped
sea salt and freshly ground black pepper

POTATO SALAD
320 g (11¼ oz) new potatoes, cooked and halved or quartered depending on size
1 small red onion, thinly sliced and blanched
2 tablespoons flat-leaf (Italian) parsley, chopped

Preheat the oven to 200°C (400°F/Gas 6).

Put the hazelnuts in a dry ovenproof frying pan and place them in the oven. Roast until they are fragrant, about 10 minutes. To remove the skins, put the hazelnuts in the centre of a clean tea towel (dish towel), enclose them on all corners and roll the nuts vigorously until the skins fall off.

In a large non-stick frying pan, heat some oil over medium heat. Season the beef with salt then sear on all sides until golden brown.

Place on a baking tray and cook in the oven for 8–12 minutes or until cooked to your liking. Rest for 10–15 minutes before slicing. (Slice against the grain.)

For the horseradish mayonnaise, combine all the ingredients in a bowl and season to taste. Set aside.

For the salad, combine the potatoes, onion, parsley and the horseradish mayonnaise in a bowl and gently toss to combine.

To serve, divide half of the watercress leaves between four serving plates, top with the potato salad, gorgonzola, roast beef slices, hazelnuts and the remaining watercress.

NOTE: The potato salad can be made a day ahead of time. Crumbed, pan-fried and sliced chicken breast fillet goes well with this salad, too.

The mushroom cream sauce is great folded through risotto towards the end of cooking. It is also terrific with other pastas such as spaghetti and fettuccine. This is a cracking dish with a salad, crusty bread and a good glass of wine.

ORECCHIETTE WITH MUSHROOMS, SPINACH & PECORINO

SERVES 4

400 g (14 oz) good-quality dried
    orecchiette pasta
extra virgin olive oil
100 g (3½ oz) pecorino cheese, shaved
small handful baby rocket (arugula)
    leaves, to garnish

MUSHROOM CREAM SAUCE
30 ml (1 fl oz) olive oil
20 g (¾ oz) unsalted butter
100 g (3½ oz) French shallots
    (eschalots), thinly sliced
5 garlic cloves, thinly sliced
1 tablespoon thyme leaves
250 g (9 oz) button mushrooms, thinly
    sliced
100 ml (3½ fl oz) dry white wine
10 g (¼ oz) dried porcini mushrooms,
    soaked in 50 ml (1½ fl oz) hot water,
    thoroughly rinsed, finely chopped
450 ml (16 fl oz) vegetable stock
300 ml (10½ fl oz) thin (pouring) cream
1 bunch English spinach, leaves washed
    and chopped
sea salt and freshly ground black pepper

Cook the pasta in a large saucepan of boiling salted water until *al dente*, drain, then toss through some olive oil. Set aside.

For the sauce, heat the oil and butter in a heavy-based frying pan over low heat and cook the shallots until soft and translucent. Add the garlic, thyme and button mushrooms and cook until the mushrooms have softened and the liquid has reduced. Add the wine and simmer until the liquid has evaporated.

Add the porcini mushrooms and stock and simmer until the liquid has reduced by half. Stir through the cream and spinach and simmer for 2–3 minutes. Remove the sauce from the heat and check the seasoning.

Serve the sauce on top of the pasta with a good sprinkle of the pecorino, a grind of black pepper and garnished with the rocket leaves.

I like to top this with toasted breadcrumbs for texture. It's delicious served with a green salad, crusty bread and a good bottle of riesling. This dish sucks up the amazing sauce quickly, so be ready to serve it as soon as it comes together.

LINGUINE WITH LOBSTER & PROSCIUTTO

SERVES 4

400 g (14 oz) good-quality dried linguine pasta

125 g (4½ oz) butter

2 garlic cloves, crushed

½ teaspoon chilli flakes

250 g (9 oz) tinned chopped tomatoes

3 prosciutto slices, julienned

sea salt and freshly ground black pepper

3 tablespoons cognac

125 ml (4 fl oz/½ cup) thin (pouring) cream

400 g (14 oz) raw lobster meat, cut into 1 cm (½ inch) chunks

10 g (¼ oz/½ cup) flat-leaf (Italian) parsley, finely chopped

Cook the pasta in a large saucepan of boiling salted water until *al dente*. Drain and set aside.

Meanwhile, put the butter, garlic and chilli in a saucepan over medium heat. As soon as the garlic begins to turn golden brown, add the tomatoes, stirring with a wooden spoon, and cook for 3 minutes. Add the prosciutto and season with salt and pepper, then cook for a further 1 minute. Sprinkle in the cognac, then add the cream and lobster meat and cook for 1–2 minutes or until the lobster is just cooked.

Add the parsley, give a final stir and toss in the pasta. Mix well and divide among four bowls.

NOTE: You could also use firm white-fleshed fish, scallops, prawns or crab meat in place of the lobster.

This is another recipe that really lends itself to toasted breadcrumbs on top and would be delicious with a side of bitter leaves such as radicchio and endive.

ORECCHIETTE IN TUNA RAGOUT

SERVES 4

400 g (14 oz) good-quality dried
  orecchiette pasta
125 ml (4 fl oz/½ cup) extra virgin
  olive oil
2 small brown onions, thinly sliced
1 garlic clove, crushed
sea salt and freshly ground black pepper
250 g (9 oz) tinned chopped tomatoes
125 ml (4 fl oz/½ cup) dry white wine
24 kalamata olives, pitted
10 g (¼ oz/½ cup) mint leaves, finely
  chopped
400 g (14 oz) fresh tuna, cut into 2 cm
  (¾ inch) dice

Cook the pasta in a large saucepan of boiling salted water until *al dente*. Drain and set aside.

Meanwhile, heat half the olive oil in a non-stick frying pan. When hot, add the onion, garlic and salt to taste and cook, stirring, for 5 minutes or until soft. Add the tomatoes and wine and simmer for a further minute or until the wine has evaporated. Add the olives and mint, shake the pan for 1 minute then remove from the heat.

In another non-stick frying pan, heat the remaining oil. When hot add the tuna and sprinkle with sea salt. Sear on all sides, about 15–20 seconds on each side. The tuna should be medium-rare in the middle.

Add the tuna to the sauce, then add the pasta. Fold through and mix thoroughly. Check the seasoning, adding lashings of pepper then divide among four bowls.

NOTE: I also like to slice the tuna in long strips, 2 cm (¾ inch) in width, sear, then slice into cubes afterwards. It allows the rareness of the tuna to shine a little more.

Angel hair pasta is very delicate and suits this dish, but by all means use spaghetti or spaghettini. You can also take the prawn tails off and chop the prawns the same size as the peas, but take care not to overcook them.

ANGEL HAIR PASTA WITH PRAWNS, PEAS & CHERVIL

SERVES 4

400 g (14 oz) dried angel hair pasta
150 ml (5 fl oz) extra virgin olive oil
3 garlic cloves, finely chopped
sea salt
700 g (1 lb 9 oz) raw king prawns
    (shrimp), peeled, deveined and tails
    intact
350 ml (12 fl oz) verjuice
350 ml (12 fl oz) thin (pouring) cream
zest of 1 lemon
80 g (2¾ oz/½ cup) fresh peas
1 teaspoon finely chopped dill
1 teaspoon finely chopped flat-leaf
    (Italian) parsley
small handful chervil sprigs, to serve

Cook the pasta in a large saucepan of boiling salted water until *al dente*. Drain, toss with 1½ tablespoons of the oil and set aside.

For the sauce, heat 80 ml (2½ fl oz/⅓ cup) of the oil in a frying pan over high heat. Add half the garlic, a good pinch of salt and the prawns and cook until the prawns have just changed colour. Remove from the pan. Add the remaining oil and garlic to the pan and cook for 30 seconds, then add the verjuice, bring to the boil and simmer for 2–3 minutes or until slightly reduced.

Add the cream, lemon zest and peas, then simmer, uncovered, for 3–4 minutes or until the sauce is slightly thickened and the peas have softened. Return the prawns to the pan and stir in the dill and parsley. Check the seasoning.

Divide the pasta among four bowls, top with the sauce and garnish with the chervil.

The chicken can be swapped for other meats. For a contrast in texture, try serving the chicken on a bed of shredded lettuce. The chicken can be roasted in the oven in the same way with the same seasoning and is delicious.

BARBECUED SPICY CHICKEN

SERVES 4, OR 8 AS PART OF A SHARED ASIAN BANQUET

1.6 kg (3 lb 8 oz) free-range or organic
   chicken
2 garlic cloves
3 cm (1¼ inch) piece fresh ginger
½ teaspoon sea salt
1 tablespoon lime juice
2 limes, cut into quarters

SPICE PASTE
2 fresh bird's-eye chillies
8 fresh long red chillies
4 red Asian shallots
2 garlic cloves
1 tomato
1 tablespoon vegetable oil
1 tablespoon fresh lime juice
1 tablespoon caster (superfine) sugar
sea salt and freshly ground white pepper

Remove the backbone from the chicken and press the chicken out flat on a board.

Pound the garlic and ginger with the salt in a mortar with a pestle. Mix in the lime juice and rub the mix into the chicken. Set aside.

For the spice paste, place the chillies, shallots, garlic and tomato in a steamer over a saucepan of boiling water and cook for 5 minutes.

Cut the chillies and tomato in half and remove the seeds, then place the steamed items in a blender and process to form a coarse mixture. Add the oil, lime juice, sugar and salt and pepper and blend to combine. Check the seasoning and balance.

Preheat a barbecue to high and cook the chicken for 5 minutes, turning halfway through.

Remove the chicken from the grill and rub it thoroughly on both sides with the spice paste. Leave for 5 minutes to allow the flavours to penetrate.

Return the chicken to the barbecue and cook for 15 minutes or until tender and golden brown on both sides and cooked through.

To serve, remove the legs from the chicken, chop each one into three and place on a serving plate. Separate the breasts, cut each breast into three pieces and place on top of the legs. Scatter the limes around.

What I love about this curry is that it is so easy: blend all the ingredients and you're ready to go. This is also a great curry for seafood, so cook the paste, add the seasoning and coconut cream and cook for about 10 minutes, then add prawns, scallops or fish. If you cook it gently it won't overcook.

CHICKEN KAPITAN

SERVES 4, OR 8 AS PART OF A SHARED ASIAN BANQUET

90 ml (3 fl oz) vegetable oil
300 g (10½ oz) spice paste (see below)
400 ml (14 fl oz) coconut cream
2 small stems lemongrass hearts, thinly
    sliced into thin rounds
800 g (1 lb 12 oz) skinless chicken thigh
    fillets, cut into 6 pieces each
400 ml (14 fl oz) coconut milk
2 tablespoons light palm sugar (jaggery)
2 tablespoons fresh lime juice

SPICE PASTE
1 tablespoon belachan (Malaysian
    shrimp paste)
2 dried red chillies, seeded and soaked
    in warm water
4 fresh long red chillies, seeded
6 red Asian shallots, chopped
4 garlic cloves, chopped
30 g (1 oz/¼ cup) chopped macadamia
    nuts
¼ teaspoon ground turmeric

Preheat the oven to 180°C (350°F/Gas 4).

For the spice paste, place the shrimp paste in a small frying pan and cook for about 10 minutes or until fragrant. Allow to cool. Place all the other spice paste ingredients, along with the shrimp paste, into a blender and blend to a fine paste.

For the curry, heat the oil in a wok over high heat. Add the spice paste and cook until fragrant, stirring frequently, for about 12 minutes, taking care not to burn it. Add half the coconut cream and the lemongrass and stir-fry until the cream separates.

Add the chicken and cook for about 6 minutes until well coated with the spice paste. Add the coconut milk and palm sugar, bring to the boil, then simmer gently for about 20 minutes until the chicken is cooked through. Add the lime juice and the remaining coconut cream. Check the balance of flavours before serving and add more palm sugar, fish sauce or lime juice as necessary.

Any leftover butter can be dotted over roasted vegetables in the last 10 minutes of cooking to make them super delicious. You could also brush it over grilled fish or chicken, or toss it through a vegetable stir-fry.

ROAST LEMONGRASS & GINGER CHICKEN

SERVES 4, OR 8 AS PART OF A SHARED ASIAN BANQUET

160 g (5¾ oz) lemongrass and ginger butter (see below)

2 x 600 g (1 lb 5 oz) double chicken breast fillets, skin on

1 tablespoon olive oil

sea salt and freshly ground pepper

sesame oil, to serve

steamed Asian greens, to serve

LEMONGRASS AND GINGER BUTTER

2 tablespoons thinly sliced lemongrass, white part only

1 tablespoon finely grated fresh ginger

1 garlic clove, chopped

2 French shallots (eschalots), peeled and diced

juice of 1 lime

1 tablespoon fish sauce

½ teaspoon caster (superfine) sugar

100 g (3½ oz) diced unsalted butter, softened to room temperature

Preheat the oven to 160°C (315°F/Gas 2–3).

For the butter, blend the lemongrass in a food processor until very fine, then add the ginger, garlic and shallots and blend again. Combine the remaining ingredients, except the butter, with the lemongrass and ginger mixture and blend until a smooth paste forms. Transfer the paste to a mixing bowl and fold through the butter. Check the seasoning.

Divide 160 g (5¾ oz) of the butter into two portions. Push each portion under the skin of each chicken breast, covering the entire area. Secure the skin at the front of the breast with toothpicks to prevent the skin shrinking during roasting. Lightly rub the chicken with the oil and season. Place the chicken on lined baking trays, breast side up.

Roast for 30 minutes or until just cooked through and the skin is golden brown. Remove from the oven and allow to cool. Discard the toothpicks.

Drizzle with sesame oil and serve with steamed Asian greens.

NOTE: You could replace the butter with 100 ml (3½ fl oz) olive oil and place it in a small saucepan with all the blended ingredients. Cook over low heat for 8–10 minutes or until fragrant.

I love Vietnamese caramel sauce. Feel free to replace the chicken with cubed pork shoulder or belly. The cooking time will be longer so you may need to add water and then allow it to evaporate during cooking. The sweetness of the caramel and the aromatic pepper is a match made in heaven.

CHICKEN WINGS IN VIETNAMESE CARAMEL SAUCE

SERVES 4, OR 8 AS PART OF A SHARED ASIAN BANQUET

75 g (2½ oz/⅓ cup) caster (superfine) sugar
3 tablespoons fish sauce
4 spring onions (scallions), thinly sliced
freshly ground black pepper
1 kg (2 lb 4 oz) chicken wings, tips removed and cut at the joint
1 tablespoon finely chopped fresh ginger

For the sauce, place the sugar in a small heavy-based saucepan over low heat and cook, swirling the pan constantly without stirring, until golden brown. Remove from the heat immediately and leave to cool for 1 minute then stir in the fish sauce (be careful as it can splatter). Return the mixture to low heat and simmer gently for 1–2 minutes, swirling the pan constantly, or until the sugar has completely dissolved. Add the spring onions and pepper and stir to combine.

Transfer the caramel sauce to a saucepan with a lid (it should be large enough to hold the chicken comfortably). Add the chicken and ginger to the sauce along with a splash of water. Stir to combine. Increase the heat to high and bring the mixture to the boil. Cover, reduce the heat to low and simmer for about 1 hour or until the chicken is tender. Check the chicken wings frequently. Skim off any excess fat.

Transfer the chicken and sauce to a serving dish and sprinkle with pepper.

Serve the chicken wings with steamed rice, stir-fried greens or an Asian-style salad, or add the wings to a banquet with a steamed fish.

This boiled curry is so easy to prepare once you make the paste. It works nicely with duck legs or pork instead of chicken, just adjust the cooking times to suit the meat.

SPICY CHICKEN STEW

SERVES 4, OR 8 AS PART OF A SHARED ASIAN BANQUET

2 tomatoes, cored and quartered

4 cinnamon sticks

5 kaffir lime leaves

1 teaspoon sea salt

600 g (1 lb 5 oz) skinless chicken thigh
    fillets (organic, if possible), thickly
    sliced

3 tablespoons grated palm sugar
    (jaggery)

2 tablespoons fish sauce

2 tablespoons tamarind water

1 small handful sweet Thai basil leaves

SPICE PASTE

3 candlenuts, roasted until golden,
    then chopped (see note)

6 fresh long red chillies, chopped

3 red Asian shallots, chopped

3 garlic cloves, chopped

2 cm (¾ inch) piece fresh ginger, peeled
    and chopped

2 cm (¾ inch) piece galangal, chopped

2 lemongrass stems, white part only,
    tough outer leaves removed,
    chopped

2–3 cm (¾–1¼ inch) piece of fresh
    turmeric, chopped

For the spice paste, pound all the ingredients together in a mortar with a pestle to a fine paste, or process the ingredients with a blender, adding a little water, if necessary.

Place the spice paste, tomatoes, cinnamon stick, lime leaves and salt in a large heavy-based saucepan. Add 1 litre (35 fl oz/4 cups) water and bring to the boil over medium heat. Reduce the heat and simmer very gently for about 1½ hours.

Add the chicken, return the sauce to the boil, then simmer for about 8 minutes or until the sauce has reduced and the chicken is cooked. Add the palm sugar, fish sauce and tamarind water, then adjust the seasoning if necessary. Stir through the basil leaves to serve.

NOTE: Candlenuts can be toxic if consumed raw, so make sure you roast them well before adding to the spice paste.

I love this chicken recipe — a great addition to any banquet alongside a curry, steamed rice and a great vegetable dish.

DEEP-FRIED CHICKEN WITH GARLIC & PEPPERCORNS

SERVES 4, OR 8 AS PART OF A SHARED ASIAN BANQUET

350 g (12 oz) skinless chicken thigh fillets (organic, if possible), cut into strips about 2 cm (¾ inch) thick
1 tablespoon fish sauce
pinch of sugar
2 coriander (cilantro) roots, scraped and chopped
pinch of sea salt
½ teaspoon white peppercorns
1 garlic bulb, cloves separated
500 ml (17 fl oz/2 cups) vegetable oil, for deep-frying
60 g (2¼ oz) plain (all-purpose) flour
freshly ground white pepper, to serve
coriander (cilantro) leaves, to serve
chilli sauce, to serve

Marinate the chicken strips in the fish sauce and sugar for 30 minutes.

Meanwhile, pound the coriander roots, salt and peppercorns in a mortar with a pestle. Add the garlic cloves and pound to a coarse paste, removing the garlic skin and hard base as you go.

Heat the oil in a wok or deep-fryer until smoking (180°C/350°F), then toss half the chicken in the flour until well coated. Shake off any excess. Deep-fry the chicken in batches, stirring regularly, for 3–4 minutes or until golden. Use a slotted spoon to remove the chicken pieces and drain on paper towel. Repeat with the remaining chicken.

Scoop out any debris from the oil and add the garlic mixture (be careful – it will spit). Move the garlic around in the oil until it is golden, then remove and drain on paper towel.

Place the fried chicken on a serving plate, sprinkle with the crisp garlic, white pepper and coriander leaves. Serve with your favourite chilli sauce.

NOTE: The chicken could instead be prawns or pieces of squid, or even firm white fish or pre-braised strips of pork belly – delicious with a Thai-style sauce such as nam jim (see page 35).

Shred any leftover chicken and use in a wrap with some of the garlic and mint yoghurt and tabouleh. Marinated lamb or thin slices of beef work well with the yoghurt as well.

SPICED CHICKEN BREAST WITH GARLIC & MINT YOGHURT

SERVES 4

185 ml (6 fl oz/¾ cup) olive oil
2 tablespoons finely chopped oregano
    leaves
1½ teaspoons ground coriander
1½ teaspoons ground cumin
large pinch of ground turmeric
pinch of chilli flakes
finely grated zest of 1 lemon (no pith)
4 x 200 g (7 oz) skinless chicken breast
    fillets, butterflied
5 garlic cloves
sea salt and freshly ground black pepper

GARLIC AND MINT YOGHURT
5 garlic cloves, halved
3 tablespoons mint leaves
400 g (14 oz) Greek-style yoghurt
sea salt and freshly ground black pepper

Preheat the oven to 180°C (350°F/Gas 4).

In a bowl, combine half the olive oil with the oregano, spices, chilli flakes and lemon zest. Add the pieces of chicken, making sure that they are all evenly coated. Marinate in the fridge for 2 hours.

For the garlic and mint yoghurt, blanch the garlic cloves in a saucepan of simmering water until soft. Drain. Blend the garlic with the mint and 100 g (3½ oz) of the yoghurt until it is a smooth paste. Fold through the remaining yoghurt and season to taste.

To cook the chicken, heat a large non-stick pan over medium–low heat. Add the remaining olive oil and the garlic cloves. Once the garlic has softened and turned a light golden colour, remove it from the pan and discard. Turn the heat up to high and add the chicken breasts, seasoning both sides with salt and pepper, and cook until golden on both sides. Place on a lined baking tray and cook in the oven for a further 4–6 minutes or until cooked through. Set aside and allow to rest.

Plate the chicken with a good dollop of the garlic and mint yoghurt.

Use the marinade on a whole roasted chicken, then cut into pieces and serve with the relish. Serve the chicken with parsnip or pumpkin purée. In spring, fresh peas are a good accompaniment.

GRILLED CHICKEN BREAST WITH CUCUMBER & YOGHURT RELISH

SERVES 4

4 chicken breast fillets, skin on

MARINADE
100 ml (3½ fl oz) extra virgin olive oil
3 fresh small red chillies, seeded and
    finely diced
1 teaspoon ground cumin
1 teaspoon ground coriander
1 teaspoon smoked paprika
1 teaspoon ground turmeric
grated zest of ½ lemon
juice of 1 lemon
2 tablespoons chopped coriander (cilantro)
sea salt

CUCUMBER AND YOGHURT RELISH
3 Lebanese (short) cucumbers, peeled,
    halved lengthways and seeded
1 celery stalk
100 ml (3½ fl oz) extra virgin olive oil
2 tablespoons red wine vinegar
1 teaspoon wholegrain mustard
sea salt and freshly ground pepper
70 g (2½ oz/¼ cup) sheep's milk or
    Greek-style yoghurt
1 vine-ripened tomato, peeled, seeded
    and roughly chopped
1 large handful mint leaves

Place each chicken breast between two sheets of baking paper and pound it gently until the fillet is about 1.5 cm (⅝ inch) thick. This will help the chicken cook evenly and quickly.

For the marinade, place all the ingredients in a food processor and process until they are well combined but not completely puréed. Marinate the chicken for 1 hour.

Meanwhile, for the relish use a sharp knife or Japanese mandolin to thinly slice the cucumber and celery. In a bowl whisk the oil, vinegar and mustard together, then season with salt and pepper to taste. Fold in the yoghurt. Add the cucumber, celery, tomato and mint and mix to combine.

Preheat a barbecue or grill pan over medium–high heat until hot. Remove the chicken from the marinade and grill it, skin side down, for 2 minutes, then turn and cook for a further 1 minute or until just cooked through. Rest in a warm place for about 1 minute.

Place the chicken pieces on a platter and serve with the relish on the side.

I love kimchi. The Koreans make it out of just about every vegetable you can imagine, however I love the one they make from cabbage the best. It is amazing in soups and stir-fries and great sliced and served with raw fish. Whatever you do, be careful not to overcook the pork – it will ruin the dish.

STIR-FRIED PORK WITH KIMCHI

SERVES 4, OR 8 AS PART OF A SHARED ASIAN BANQUET

2 tablespoons vegetable oil
600 g (1 lb 5 oz) deboned pork belly,
    skin on, sliced into 5 mm (¼ inch)
    thick slices
sea salt and freshly ground white pepper
150 g (5½ oz) kimchi (available at
    good Asian grocers), cut into 4 cm
    (1½ inch) pieces
4 spring onions (scallions), cut into
    batons
1 garlic clove, finely chopped
½ teaspoon ground chilli powder
½ teaspoon Asian sesame sauce
    (available at good Asian grocers)
½ teaspoon roasted sesame seeds
7 g (⅛ oz/¼ cup) coriander (cilantro)
    leaves
steamed rice, to serve

Heat the oil in a wok over high heat until just smoking. Add the pork, then season with salt and pepper. Cook over high heat for 10 minutes or until browned, being careful not to overcook it.

Add the kimchi, spring onion, garlic, chilli powder, sesame sauce and 1 tablespoon water and cook briefly to incorporate.

Divide the pork among serving bowls and sprinkle with the sesame seeds and coriander. Serve with steamed rice.

NOTE: You can also use sliced chicken thighs or a firm white-fleshed fish such as blue-eye trevalla.

You can replace the water chestnuts with bamboo shoots or lotus root if you like, or use some of all three for a different taste and texture experience.

BRAISED PORK WITH WATER CHESTNUTS

SERVES 8–12 AS PART OF A SHARED ASIAN BANQUET

125 ml (4 fl oz/½ cup) oyster sauce
30 g (1 oz/¼ cup) grated palm sugar
(jaggery)
1 fresh long red chilli, sliced into rounds
290 g (10¼ oz) tinned water chestnuts,
drained and quartered
1 kg (2 lb 4 oz) pork neck
sea salt and freshly ground black pepper
steamed rice and Asian greens, to serve

Preheat the oven to 160°C (315°F/Gas 2–3).

Place the oyster sauce, palm sugar, chilli, water chestnuts and 500 ml (17 fl oz/2 cups) water in a medium saucepan. Bring to the boil over high heat then reduce the heat to medium–low and simmer until the sugar dissolves.

Place the pork neck in a deep casserole dish just large enough to hold the piece of pork and pour the oyster sauce mixture over the meat.

Cover with foil and bake for 2–3 hours, turning every half hour (you may need to add extra water if the liquid reduces too much). Remove the foil and cook for a further 20–30 minutes or until the meat is tender and the sauce is reduced. Check the seasoning.

Slice the pork and serve with coconut or plain steamed rice and Asian greens.

NOTE: To make coconut rice, replace a quarter of the water needed for cooking with coconut milk.

If peaches are in season, you could use them in place of the figs. I like to serve the pork with mustard fruits. Peas and spinach go well with this, and pumpkin, yam or potato purée are, in the words of English cricketing legend Mark Nicholas, 'Smashing, baby'.

ROAST RACK OF PORK WITH FRESH FIG

SERVES 4

4-bone rack of pork, skin on, chine removed (see note)
sea salt and freshly ground pepper
4 fresh figs
500 ml (17 fl oz/2 cups) vegetable oil
good-quality aged balsamic vinegar
extra virgin olive oil

The night before cooking, use a very sharp knife or one-sided razor blade to make cuts in the pork skin from top to bottom, running in the same direction as the bones, about 3 mm (⅛ inch) apart (don't go too deep into the flesh). Rub sea salt into the skin. Place the rack in the fridge overnight, uncovered, to dry the skin and promote crunchy crackling.

The next day, preheat the oven to 180°C (350°F/Gas 4). Place the pork on a wire rack in a roasting tin and roast, undisturbed, for 30 minutes. Reduce the oven temperature to 160°C (315°F/Gas 2–3), add the figs and bake for 30 minutes or until the meat's core temperature reaches about 71°C (160°F). When done, turn the oven temperature down to about 60°C (140°F). (Leave the door ajar to hasten cooling, if you like.)

Rest the meat in the cool oven for about 30 minutes. Check the meat's core temperature again; it should be about 75°C (167°F).

Just before serving, heat the vegetable oil in a small saucepan until just smoking. Remove the roasting tin from the oven and use a spoon to pour the hot oil carefully over the pork skin to complete the crackling.

Place the meat on a chopping board and cut into four cutlets. Place each cutlet on a serving plate with a fig. Sprinkle with salt and pepper, drizzle with the balsamic and olive oil and serve immediately.

NOTE: The chine bone is the bone that runs down the centre of the meat; the 't' in t-bone. Have your butcher remove this.

The horseradish butter in this recipe is also delicious with grilled chicken and salad.

BEEF FILLET WITH HORSERADISH BUTTER & GRILLED MUSHROOMS

SERVES 4

800 g (1 lb 12 oz) beef fillet
sea salt and freshly ground black pepper
extra virgin olive oil
4 large flat mushrooms, stems trimmed

HORSERADISH BUTTER

1 tablespoon finely grated fresh
   horseradish (or good-quality jarred)
small handful flat-leaf (Italian) parsley
   leaves, roughly chopped
3 teaspoons dijon mustard
juice of 1 lemon
freshly ground white pepper
250 g (9 oz) room-temperature butter,
   chopped

LEMON THYME OIL

½ bunch lemon thyme, leaves picked
   and finely chopped
1 garlic clove, finely chopped
150 ml (5 fl oz) extra virgin olive oil
sea salt and freshly ground white pepper

Preheat the oven to 200°C (400°F/Gas 6).

For the horseradish butter, use a food processor to mix the horseradish, parsley, mustard, lemon juice and a pinch of white pepper for about 1 minute or until well combined. Add the butter and process for a further 30 seconds or until just combined. Roll the butter mixture in sheets of baking paper into a log shape about 4 cm (1½ inches) in diameter. Refrigerate until firm.

Season the beef with salt and pepper. Heat a heavy-based frying pan over high heat and add a splash of olive oil. Seal the beef on all sides until browned. Bake in the oven for 10–15 minutes or until desired doneness (see below). Allow to rest for 10–15 minutes before slicing.

For the lemon thyme oil, mix all the ingredients in a bowl until combined. Season to taste.

In a non-stick frying pan, heat half of the lemon thyme oil and add the mushrooms, stem side down. Cook for 3–4 minutes over medium heat until golden. Turn over, and brush the insides of the mushrooms with the remaining lemon thyme oil and cook until the mushrooms are tender.

Serve the beef sliced with a disc of the horseradish butter and a grilled mushroom.

NOTE: Use a meat thermometer to cook the beef. When the temperature of the beef is 52°C (125°F), rest it for 10–15 minutes for rare. Rest at 55°C (131°F) for medium rare and 60°C (140°F) for well done.

BEEF TAGINE

SERVES 8–12

800 g (1 lb 12 oz) beef fillet, cut into 2 cm
(¾ inch) dice
extra virgin olive oil
1 red onion, cut into 6 pieces
2 carrots, cut into 4 cm (1½ inch) long
pieces
1 sweet potato, peeled and cut into 4 cm
(1½ inch) pieces
12 green beans
60 g (2¼ oz) whole blanched almonds
sea salt
2 tablespoons honey
juice of 1 lemon
8 fresh dates, pitted
70 g (2½ oz) black olives, pitted
¼ preserved lemon, pith removed and
zest finely chopped
2 tablespoons coriander (cilantro) leaves
2 tablespoons flat-leaf (Italian) parsley
leaves
steamed couscous, to serve

CHERMOULA
1 red onion, roughly chopped
4 garlic cloves, roughly chopped
1 bunch coriander (cilantro), roughly
chopped
1 bunch flat-leaf (Italian) parsley, roughly
chopped
1 heaped teaspoon sea salt
1 tablespoon ground cumin
1 tablespoon ground coriander
1½ tablespoons ground chilli powder
1 tablespoon ground turmeric
2 teaspoons sweet paprika
1½ tablespoons ras el hanout (North
African spice mix)
185 ml (6 fl oz/¾ cup) extra virgin olive oil
juice of 1 lemon

For the chermoula, place all the ingredients in a food processor, except the oil and lemon juice. Process for 20 seconds, then slowly pour in the oil to form a thick paste. Stir through the lemon juice. Set aside 1 cup for the tagine.

Combine 2 tablespoons of the chermoula with the beef and set aside to marinate for 1 hour.

In a tagine or a large saucepan with a tight-fitting lid, heat a little oil and the rest of the reserved chermoula over medium heat. Add the onion, carrot, sweet potato, beans, almonds and a little salt and sauté for 2 minutes. Add enough water to half cover the vegetables, then add the honey and lemon juice and cover. Reduce the heat to a very gentle simmer and cook for about 30 minutes. Remove the lid and turn the ingredients carefully. Add the dates and olives. Cover the pan again and cook for a further 30 minutes or until the vegetables are tender.

Heat a frying pan over high heat until hot and add a little oil. When smoking, add the beef and quickly sauté to colour and seal on all sides.

Spoon the beef into the tagine and mix well. You can serve the dish in the tagine or saucepan, spooned onto a large platter or divide among plates. Just before serving, sprinkle with the preserved lemon zest and the herbs. Serve with couscous.

NOTES: This is a luxurious version of a tagine. Normally you braise a cheaper braising cut of meat until tender. You can do that but you'll need to add more water and cook for about 2 hours. The quantities given for the chermoula make 2 cups. Store the leftovers in the fridge for a week or two. Spread over fish and sear in a frying pan for a great blackened and tasty meal. For quick preserved lemons, boil whole lemons in very salty water (saltier than seawater) for 20 minutes. Remove and when cool, quarter the lemons, discard the pulp and pith and chop the zest. Store the zest in a jar, covered with a layer of oil.

Frozen peas work perfectly here. They are much more reliable than fresh, other than in spring when it is worth the effort to pod them. The vegetables are yummy with roast chicken, veal or lamb. Or you could use fillet steak and make a quick and easy minute steak with it.

GRILLED BEEF RIB-EYE WITH PEAS & ROASTED CHERRY TOMATOES

SERVES 4

4 x 360 g (12¾ oz) beef rib-eye steaks
sea salt and freshly ground black pepper
500 g (1 lb 12 oz) cherry tomatoes on the
    vine
olive oil, for greasing
1 bunch thyme, leaves picked
3 garlic cloves
extra virgin olive oil
400 g (14 oz) frozen peas

Remove the meat from the fridge 2 hours before you intend to start cooking and season liberally with sea salt.

For the tomatoes, preheat the oven to 200°C (400°F/Gas 6). Place the tomatoes in an oiled roasting tin.

Scatter over the thyme and garlic, drizzle with 3 tablespoons of oil and season with salt and pepper. Roast for 10 minutes or until the skins are beginning to blister and soften.

In the meantime, bring a saucepan of water to the boil and salt heavily. Boil the peas for 2 minutes then drain.

Pour the peas over the roasted tomatoes and stir to combine. Season with pepper.

Preheat a barbecue or grill (broiler) to high. Rub the beef with a little oil.

For criss-cross grill marks, place the beef on the grill bars and cook for 3 minutes. Rotate the beef 90 degrees and cook for a further 3 minutes, turn the beef over and cook for a further 5 minutes. Place the beef on a plate, cover with foil to keep warm and allow to rest for 10 minutes.

Spoon the tomato and peas into the middle of four serving plates, then place the beef in the centre.

Sprinkle with salt and pepper to serve.

Panko crumbs are large Japanese breadcrumbs available at supermarkets these days. They give a wonderful crunchy light texture. For an extra caramelised flavour, fry the eggplant with the skin on until golden brown before mashing through the tomato sauce.

CRUMBED VEAL STEAKS WITH EGGPLANT & TOMATO SALAD

SERVES 4

4 x 150 g (5½ oz) thin veal leg steaks
plain (all-purpose) flour
3 eggs, organic, if possible, lightly
    whisked
180 g (6 oz/3 cups) Japanese
    breadcrumbs (panko)
sea salt and freshly ground black pepper
1 lemon, cut into quarters
extra virgin olive oil, for frying

EGGPLANT AND TOMATO SALAD
750 g (1 lb 10 oz) eggplants (aubergines)
500 g (1 lb 2 oz) tomatoes, peeled and
    chopped
5 garlic cloves, chopped
80 ml (2½ fl oz/⅓ cup) extra virgin
    olive oil
½ teaspoon smoked paprika
pinch of ground chilli powder
1 teaspoon ground cumin
1 bunch flat-leaf (Italian) parsley, roughly
    chopped
1 bunch coriander (cilantro), roughly
    chopped
1 handful pitted black olives
juice of 1 lemon

For the salad, preheat the oven to 240°C (475°F/Gas 8). Prick the eggplants all over with a fork, wrap in foil, then roast in the oven for 50 minutes or until very soft. When cool enough to handle, peel, then place in a strainer and press out as much juice as possible. Chop into large chunks.

In a non-stick frying pan, cook the tomatoes and garlic with 2 tablespoons of the olive oil and a little sea salt over low heat for about 20 minutes or until reduced to a thick sauce. Mix with the eggplant, then add the spices, herbs, olives, lemon juice and the remaining olive oil and season to taste.

Place the veal steaks between two pieces of plastic wrap. Use a rolling pin to pound each steak to about 5 mm (¼ inch) thick. Coat a veal steak in flour, shake off the excess, then dip it in the egg, then the breadcrumbs. Shake off the excess. Repeat with the remaining steaks.

In a large non-stick frying pan, heat 2–3 tablespoons of oil per steak over medium heat. In batches, fry the crumbed veal steaks until golden brown. (Keep the cooked ones warm in a 70°C/150°F/Gas ¼ oven.)

Serve the veal with a dollop of eggplant salad, a sprinkle of sea salt, a good grind of pepper and lemon wedges.

NOTE: Crumbed lamb cutlets, chicken or fish – even king prawns – are damn tasty with this eggplant salad.

I love this served with a simple rocket and parmesan salad, mashed potato or cherry tomatoes and buffalo mozzarella.

VEAL ESCALOPES WITH ARTICHOKES & PROSCIUTTO

SERVES 4

½ lemon

4 globe artichokes

plain (all-purpose) flour, for dusting

sea salt and freshly ground black pepper

8 x 120 g (4¼ oz) thin slices veal tenderloin, trimmed

120 ml (4 fl oz) olive oil

3 garlic cloves, finely chopped

170 ml (5½ fl oz/⅔ cup) white wine

8 thin prosciutto slices

1 tarragon sprig, leaves roughly chopped

Preheat the oven to 150°C (300°F/Gas 2).

Squeeze the lemon into a bowl of cold water. Trim the artichokes of their tough outer leaves and trim the stem, leaving 3 cm (1¼ inches) attached. Use a vegetable peeler or a small knife to remove the tough green outer layer of the stem. Cut the artichokes in half lengthways and scrape out the choke (the furry centre) and discard. Drop the artichoke halves in the lemon water to stop discolouration. Drain and pat dry with paper towel.

Place a little flour in a small bowl and season with salt and pepper. Dust each piece of veal with the seasoned flour and set aside.

Heat half the oil in a saucepan. Add the artichokes, garlic and a little salt and pepper. Sauté for 5 minutes or until the garlic is fragrant and the artichokes are browned. Add 170 ml (5½ fl oz/⅔ cup) water, bring to a simmer, cover and cook for 10 minutes or until the artichokes are soft and liquid is almost evaporated. Set aside.

In a non-stick frying pan, heat a little oil over medium heat and pan-fry the veal in batches for 1–2 minutes on each side, or until browned. When you have cooked the last piece of veal, set them aside in the oven to keep warm.

Add the wine to the pan to deglaze. Add the prosciutto and tarragon and simmer for 1–2 minutes to just wilt the prosciutto. Add the artichokes and a few tablespoons of water to create a sauce. Check the seasoning. Let it bubble for up to 30 seconds, then serve immediately over the veal, on four individual plates or one large serving platter.

NOTE: Flattened skinless chicken breast fillet is a good substitute for the veal.

Try to use really good bread. It's the basis of any great sandwich. This is great with a cooked crumbed chicken breast or some shredded roast chicken.

STEAK SANDWICH WITH COLESLAW & TOMATO CHILLI RELISH

SERVES 4

4 x 100 g (3½ oz) beef fillets
2 tablespoons extra virgin olive oil
sea salt and freshly ground black pepper
8 slices of sourdough, toasted until golden
1 garlic clove, peeled
40 g (1½ oz) baby rocket (arugula) leaves

TOMATO CHILLI RELISH
4 ripe tomatoes
1 tablespoon extra virgin olive oil
½ small brown onion, finely chopped
1 garlic clove, finely chopped
½ red capsicum (pepper), seeded and
    cut into 1 cm (½ inch) dice
1 teaspoon finely chopped fresh ginger
100 ml (3½ fl oz) cider vinegar
2 tablespoons caster (superfine) sugar
2 tablespoons brown sugar
1 tablespoon fresh lemon juice
½ teaspoon sea salt
3 fresh bird's-eye chillies, finely chopped

COLESLAW
small wedge white cabbage, finely shaved
small wedge red cabbage, finely shaved
2 teaspoons sea salt
100 g (3½ oz) whole-egg mayonnaise
juice of 1 lemon
1 small handful flat-leaf (Italian) parsley
    leaves, finely chopped
sea salt and freshly cracked black pepper

For the relish, blanch the tomatoes in boiling water for 10 seconds, then refresh quickly in iced water. Peel, halve, remove seeds and chop into 2 cm (¾ inch) pieces.

Heat the oil in a large heavy-based frying pan. Add the onion, garlic, capsicum and ginger and stir over low heat until the onion is soft and lightly browned. Add the remaining ingredients to the pan and simmer, uncovered, stirring occasionally for about 1 hour or until the mixture thickens, being careful that the relish does not stick to the base.

For the coleslaw, combine both cabbages with the salt. Mix well and allow to sit for 30 minutes or until the cabbage has started to wilt and soften. Rinse and drain well. Combine with the mayonnaise, lemon juice and parsley and season to taste.

Use a meat mallet to pound each steak gently to a 3–4 mm (⅛–¼ inch) thickness. Brush each steak with the oil and season with salt and pepper. Heat a chargrill or non-stick frying pan and grill the steak for 1–2 minutes on each side. Rest the steaks for 5 minutes.

Toast or chargrill the bread until golden then rub with the garlic clove.

To serve, place a slice of toasted sourdough on a plate, top with some coleslaw, a steak, rocket leaves and a generous spoonful of tomato chilli relish and finish with a second slice of sourdough.

NOTE: For a lighter slaw, replace the mayonnaise with red wine vinegar and extra virgin olive oil. You can increase or decrease the chilli in the relish if preferred. If you want to make it even simpler, use a bought chilli or barbecue sauce.

These babies are cracking served with a steak sandwich.

SWEET POTATO WEDGES

SERVES 8–12 AS A SIDE DISH

800 g (1 lb 12 oz) peeled sweet potato, cut into 6–8 cm (2½–3¼ inch) wedges
3 tablespoons olive oil
2 tablespoons rosemary leaves, finely chopped
1 tablespoon thyme leaves, finely chopped
sea salt and freshly ground black pepper

Preheat the oven to 200°C (400°F/Gas 6).

In a large bowl, combine all the ingredients and toss to coat well. Place the wedges, facing up, on a baking tray lined with baking paper. Bake for 30–40 minutes or until cooked through and golden.

Drain on paper towel and serve.

You can replace the beans with in-season asparagus, snow peas or bok choy.

STIR-FRIED SNAKE BEANS

SERVES 6–8 AS A SIDE DISH

2 tablespoons vegetable oil
500 g (1 lb 2 oz) snake (yard-long) beans,
    cut into 6 cm (2½ inch) lengths
4 garlic cloves, finely chopped
2 teaspoons caster (superfine) sugar
1½ tablespoons fish sauce
1½ tablespoons chicken stock
sea salt and freshly ground black pepper,
    to serve

Heat the oil in a wok over medium–high heat until it starts to smoke. Add the beans and stir-fry for about 1 minute. Add the garlic and stir-fry until fragrant. Add the sugar, fish sauce and stock and stir-fry for another 30 seconds or until the liquid is slightly reduced. Check seasoning before serving.

The cutlets can be barbecued or grilled under an oven grill. They should be well done and crispy. I love them with couscous as well. The pumpkin purée is amazing with roast chicken and it is also wonderful with barbecued fish, so keep it in mind for other dishes – a truly adaptable accompaniment. I like to serve these cutlets with a simple salad such as shaved cabbage dressed with extra virgin olive oil and balsamic vinegar.

MARINATED LAMB CUTLETS WITH PUMPKIN PUREE

SERVES 4

1 teaspoon whole fennel seeds

1 teaspoon whole coriander seeds

½ teaspoon cardamom seeds

½ teaspoon sea salt, plus ½ teaspoon extra

1 handful coriander (cilantro) leaves, chopped

1 handful mint leaves, chopped

½ teaspoon ground chilli powder

1 teaspoon ground turmeric

2 teaspoons garam masala

1 tablespoon fresh lemon juice

3 tablespoons plain yoghurt

12 trimmed lamb cutlets

oil, for greasing

PUMPKIN PUREE

400 g (14 oz) peeled pumpkin (winter squash), cut into 4 cm (1½ inch) dice

50 g (1¾ oz) unsalted butter, softened

3 teaspoons extra virgin olive oil

sea salt and freshly ground black pepper

In a non-stick frying pan, roast the fennel, coriander and cardamom seeds over medium heat until fragrant. Use a spice grinder, or a mortar with a pestle, to grind the roasted seeds and salt to a fine powder.

In a separate bowl, mix the coriander and mint leaves with the extra salt, the roasted seeds, chilli, turmeric, garam masala, lemon juice and yoghurt until well combined. Marinate the cutlets in the spiced yoghurt mixture in the fridge for about 2 hours.

To make the pumpkin, steam the pumpkin for 20–30 minutes or until very tender. Purée in a blender with the butter and oil until smooth. Season with salt and pepper to taste.

Heat a large well-oiled frying pan over medium–high heat. Cook the cutlets on each side for 2–3 minutes or until done to your liking.

Allow the cutlets to rest for a few minutes then serve immediately on a platter, with the pumpkin purée on the side.

A pea, asparagus and potato salad also works well with these cutlets. Aïoli is also a great accompaniment, as is mayonnaise mixed with chilli. Brush the cutlets with the mint jelly and serve on a large platter for a party. You'll need to start the mint sauce a day ahead.

BARBECUED LAMB CUTLETS WITH MINT JELLY

SERVES 4

12 trimmed lamb cutlets
1 tablespoon extra virgin olive oil, for
    brushing
sea salt and freshly ground black pepper
steamed peas and blanched asparagus,
    to serve
mint leaves, to serve

MINT JELLY
3 large granny smith apples, quartered,
    cores and stems removed
20 g (¾ oz/1 cup) mint leaves, plus 5 g
    (⅛ oz/¼ cup), finely chopped, extra
250 ml (9 fl oz/1 cup) white wine vinegar
220 g (7¾ oz/1 cup) caster (superfine)
    sugar

To make the mint sauce, place the apples and 250 ml (9 fl oz/1 cup) water in a large saucepan over medium heat. Cover and simmer for 20 minutes or until softened. Place the mint and the vinegar in a blender and blend until finely chopped. Add it to the apples and simmer for 5 minutes.

Remove from the heat and set aside for 2 hours to allow the flavours to infuse. Place the apple and mint mixture in a fine sieve and sit it in a suitable bowl. Cover, place in the fridge and allow the juices to filter through overnight.

The next day, measure out 250 ml (9 fl oz/1 cup) of the juices and place in a saucepan over high heat. Add the sugar and stir until dissolved. Bring to the boil, reduce the heat to a simmer, and cook for 15–20 minutes, skimming the scum from the surface regularly, until reduced and thickened to a syrupy consistency. Remove from the heat and cool, then refrigerate overnight to become jelly.

Preheat a barbecue chargrill plate to high.

Lightly brush the cutlets with olive oil and season. Cook for 3–4 minutes each side, then set aside and rest for 5–10 minutes.

Serve the cutlets on a bed of peas and asparagus, with mint leaves scattered over and the mint sauce on the side.

Tabouleh makes a super-refreshing accompaniment. The skordalia is great with seafood, and I love it on a slice of sourdough.

ZA'ATAR-CRUSTED LAMB FILLET WITH SKORDALIA

SERVES 4

3 tablespoons za'atar (see notes)
1 tablespoon sumac (see notes)
125 ml (4 fl oz/½ cup) olive oil
4 lamb backstraps, trimmed
sea salt and freshly ground black pepper

SKORDALIA
3 garlic bulbs
800 g (1 lb 12 oz) all-purpose potatoes
    (eg desiree), peeled, cut into 3 cm
    (1¼ inch) dice
3 tablespoons almond meal
1 tablespoon boiling water
75 ml (2¼ fl oz) good-quality olive oil
juice of ½ lemon
sea salt and freshly ground white pepper

Combine the za'atar, sumac and the oil and mix to a paste. Place the lamb in a bowl, add the paste and toss to coat. Cover and refrigerate for at least 1 hour.

Preheat the oven to 150°C (300°F/Gas 2).

For the skordalia, wrap the garlic bulbs separately in foil and roast for 20–30 minutes or until the garlic is very soft. Cut each bulb in half crossways and squeeze out the garlic into a bowl, then mash with a fork until puréed.

Steam the potato until very tender and pass through a mouli or ricer into a large bowl. Stir in the roasted garlic purée, almond meal and boiling water. Slowly add the olive oil in a stream until incorporated. Add the lemon juice and season to taste.

Remove the lamb from the fridge and bring to room temperature. Season well, then pan-fry or chargrill over medium–high heat for 5–8 minutes or until preferred doneness. Remove from the pan and rest for 5–10 minutes before serving.

NOTES: Za'atar is a Middle Eastern herb and spice mix consisting mainly of dried oregano, salt and sesame seeds. It's great in crusts and marinades and fantastic with yoghurt as a dip for bread. Sumac is a red berry that, when ground, has a pleasing citrus lemony sour taste. It also adds great colour.

I adore the wonderful Mediterranean flavours with this lamb leg but you can keep it even more simple serving the marinated lamb with roast or boiled vegetables. You can also replace the chickpeas with tinned or cooked white beans or lentils. The lamb leg can also be roasted in the oven with the same flavourings.

MARINATED LAMB LEG WITH CHICKPEA SALAD & GARLIC YOGHURT DRESSING

SERVES 4–6

1.5 kg (3 lb 5 oz) boneless leg of lamb
1 lemon

MARINADE
2 tablespoons chopped flat-leaf (Italian)
    parsley
1 teaspoon chopped thyme
2 tablespoons chopped oregano
3 garlic cloves, finely chopped
125 ml (4 fl oz/½ cup) extra virgin olive oil
1 teaspoon finely grated lemon zest
sea salt

GARLIC YOGHURT DRESSING
250 g (9 oz) sheep's milk yoghurt
2 garlic cloves, finely chopped
juice of 1 lemon
sea salt and freshly ground pepper

CHICKPEA SALAD
300 g (10½ oz) tinned chickpeas,
    drained and rinsed
1 garlic clove, crushed
½ teaspoon ground chilli powder
3 tablespoons extra virgin olive oil
juice of 1 lemon
sea salt and freshly ground pepper

Lay the lamb flat on a board, skin side down, and cut the two large muscles almost in half so you can open them up. You should have a rectangle of lamb about 3 cm (1¼ inches) thick. (You can ask your butcher to do this for you.)

For the marinade, place all the ingredients in a large bowl and mix well. Add the lamb and turn a few times to coat. Cover and refrigerate for 6 hours or overnight, turning occasionally.

Remove the lamb from the fridge several hours before cooking.

For the garlic yoghurt dressing, combine all the ingredients in a bowl and mix well.

For the chickpea salad, combine all the ingredients in a bowl and stir to coat the chickpeas.

Preheat a grill (broiler) or barbecue to medium–high. Place the lamb on the barbecue and pour the marinade over the meat. Cook for 8 minutes, then turn and cook for a further 8 minutes. Transfer the lamb to a plate to rest in a warm place for 10 minutes. Carve into slices.

To serve, place some chickpea salad on each plate, and top with the sliced lamb. Add a dollop of yoghurt and a squeeze of lemon, and spoon any juices over the top.

The Indian flavours in this simple meal are wonderful. The yoghurt sauce goes well with just about everything – from chicken to seafood.

BARBECUED LAMB CUTLETS WITH SPICY YOGHURT SAUCE

SERVES 4

125 ml (4 fl oz/½ cup) vegetable oil

310 g (11 oz/2 cups) finely chopped onions

sea salt

3 garlic cloves, finely chopped

2 tablespoons finely chopped fresh ginger

¼ teaspoon ground turmeric

¼ teaspoon ground cinnamon

¼ teaspoon ground cloves

260 g (9¼ oz/1 cup) plain yoghurt

12 trimmed lamb cutlets

2 tablespoons coriander (cilantro) leaves

2 tablespoons mint leaves

1 fresh long green chilli, seeded and finely chopped

1 fresh long red chilli, seeded and finely chopped

Place half the oil in a medium saucepan and heat gently. Add the onion and a pinch of sea salt and cook for 15–20 minutes (stirring constantly so the onion doesn't stick and burn) or until it turns light brown.

Add the garlic and ginger and cook for a further minute or so. Add the turmeric, cinnamon and cloves, stir for a moment, then add the yoghurt and remove from the heat.

Transfer the onion mixture to a blender and purée until smooth. Keep warm.

Heat a barbecue or grill (broiler) to medium–high. Season the cutlets with salt and brush with the remaining oil. Grill the lamb for 3 minutes on each side or until cooked to your liking. Rest the lamb for 3–5 minutes in a warm place, then pile the lamb on a plate and sprinkle with the coriander, mint and chillies. Serve the yoghurt sauce on the side.

The marinade works well with lamb leg or shoulder, chicken or pork. I do love lamb with parsnip purée but yam or pumpkin are quite special too.

SPICY MARJORAM & THYME-MARINATED CUTLETS WITH PARSNIP PUREE

SERVES 4

12 trimmed lamb cutlets
2 garlic cloves, finely chopped
1 teaspoon sea salt
2 tablespoons chopped marjoram
1 tablespoon chopped thyme
3 tablespoons chopped flat-leaf (Italian) parsley
1 tablespoon ground cumin
½ teaspoon chilli flakes
3 tablespoons extra virgin olive oil, plus extra
freshly ground black pepper
lemon wedges

PARSNIP PUREE
60 g (2¼ oz) unsalted butter, chopped, plus extra
2 tablespoons extra virgin olive oil
1 small brown onion, finely diced
2 garlic cloves, finely chopped
4 parsnips, peeled, cored and diced
chicken stock (or water), to just cover
sea salt and freshly ground black pepper
juice of 1 lemon, or to taste

Remove the cutlets from the fridge 1 hour before cooking.

For the parsnip purée, place the butter and oil in a saucepan with a lid over medium–low heat and cook the onion and garlic slowly, without colouring, for 8 minutes or until soft and sweet. Add the parsnip and cook for a further 5 minutes, then add the stock and simmer for 30–45 minutes or until most of the liquid has evaporated. Season well, then blend to a smooth purée, adding more butter if necessary. Add lemon juice to your liking. Set aside and keep warm.

For the marinade, pound the garlic and salt to a paste in a mortar with a pestle. Add the herbs and pound for a further 2 minutes. Add the cumin, chilli flakes and oil and stir until completely incorporated.

Mix the cutlets with the marinade on a plate and leave for 1 hour to infuse.

Preheat a barbecue to medium–high, then place the cutlets on the hottest part. Cook for 2 minutes on one side, then turn over and cook for a further 1–2 minutes or until done to your liking. Transfer to a plate, cover with foil and set aside in a warm place.

Place three cutlets on each plate, mix a little extra olive oil with the juices from the resting plate and pour over the cutlets. Give a good grind of pepper. Place a spoonful of parsnip purée on each plate (or serve it in a bowl in the middle of the table).

Finish with lemon wedges on the side.

NOTE: You can change the marinade to suit your tastes. Add whatever herbs or spices you like – clove and cardamom can be a bit overpowering – and remember to keep it balanced so it tastes good. Increase or reduce the chilli to suit too.

ASIAN BANQUET

I have chosen a few of my favourite Asian dishes that work well together in a shared banquet style. As with the rest of the recipes in this book, the strength of the dish lies in using quality, fresh ingredients. Add some Asian-style seasoning and you're set. Home cooks often feel this type of cooking is beyond them, but nothing could be further from the truth. Start with a couple of the easier recipes and build on your experience and soon you will be sending four or five dishes to the table with a lovely bowl of steamed rice. Pick and choose your Asian dishes so they balance well together – something steamed, something stir-fried and perhaps a braise, and mix up the proteins. Plenty of other Asian dishes in this book work well in a banquet too – feel free to substitute the following dishes with your favourites.

You could fry poached chicken wings until crisp and serve with the hoisin dressing. Or pour the dressing over fried crumbed skinless chicken breast fillet strips and steamed rice. One-bowl food – very satisfying.

EGG NOODLE SALAD WITH BARBECUE DUCK & HOISIN SAUCE

SERVES 4, OR 8 AS PART OF A SHARED ASIAN BANQUET

300 g (10½ oz) fresh thick egg noodles
vegetable oil
2 spring onions (scallions), julienned
2 Lebanese (short) cucumbers, peeled, seeded and julienned
115 g (4 oz/1 cup) bean sprouts, tails trimmed
7 g (⅛ oz/1 small bunch) enoki mushrooms, bases trimmed, separated
25 g (1 oz/½ cup) roughly chopped coriander (cilantro) leaves
5 g (⅛ oz/¼ cup) garlic chives, cut into 1 cm (½ inch) lengths
300 g (10½ oz) shredded duck meat, skin on

DRESSING
3 tablespoons Chinkiang black vinegar
250 ml (9 fl oz/1 cup) hoisin sauce
2 tablespoons sesame oil

For the dressing, combine all the ingredients in a bowl and mix well. Check the balance is right.

Soak the noodles in boiling water until *al dente*. Drain and refresh in cold water and drain again. Toss with a little vegetable oil.

Combine the noodles with all the vegetables and herbs, the duck meat and the dressing and toss to combine.

To serve, divide among four bowls, or one large plate for a shared meal.

NOTE: Roast chicken or cooked prawns are a good substitute for the duck and if you don't have egg noodles handy, just use spaghetti.

Replace the squid with steamed prawns or fish, roast chicken or a barbecued and sliced beef or pork fillet. Add some pounded coriander roots to the dressing to lift the flavour. Tamarind can be bought either in water form ready to go, or as a pulp where you soak it in hot water then strain. Or you can add more lime juice or replace the tamarind with rice wine vinegar.

THAI-STYLE SQUID SALAD

SERVES 2, OR 4 AS PART OF A SHARED ASIAN BANQUET

300 g (10½ oz) cleaned squid
3 red Asian shallots, thinly sliced
1 kaffir lime leaf, julienned
½ lemongrass stem, pale part
    only, tough outer leaves
    removed, julienned
1 small handful mixed coriander
    (cilantro), mint and Thai basil leaves

DRESSING
4 wild green chillies, thinly sliced (see
    note)
1 tablespoon caster (superfine) sugar
juice of 1 lime
2 tablespoons tamarind water
2 tablespoons fish sauce

For the dressing, pound the chillies and sugar in a mortar with a pestle to form a paste. Stir in the lime juice, tamarind water and fish sauce and check the seasoning.

To prepare the squid, cut off the tentacles and cut down the centre of the squid so it will open out flat. Score the inside with a criss-cross pattern then slice lengthways into 2 cm (¾ inch) wide strips. Cut the tentacles in half.

Blanch the squid in a large saucepan of boiling salted water for about 30 seconds or until it just turns opaque. Drain and allow to cool.

Toss the squid, shallots, lime leaf, lemongrass and herbs together in a bowl. Add the dressing, gently toss again and serve.

NOTE: Wild green chillies of Thailand are also known as bird's eye chillies or heavenly rat droppings! The chillies have a wonderful immediate heat and a citrus lime flavour.

There are lots of ingredients here but they are simple to put together. Coriander is a nice addition at the end. I like to serve this with boiled yam, potatoes or pumpkin.

HOT & SOUR OXTAIL

SERVES 4, OR 6–8 AS PART OF A SHARED ASIAN BANQUET

10 French shallots

10 garlic cloves

8 dried long red chillies, seeded and roughly chopped (see notes)

2 tablespoons ground cumin

1 teaspoon ground turmeric

2 lemongrass stems, pale part only, tough outer stem removed, roughly chopped

4 cm (1½ inch) piece fresh galangal, roughly chopped

2 kg (4 lb 8 oz) oxtail (see notes)

5 kaffir lime leaves, crushed

400 ml (14 fl oz) tamarind water

3 tablespoons grated palm sugar (jaggery)

3 tablespoons tomato paste (concentrated purée)

sea salt and freshly ground pepper

steamed rice, to serve

In a blender, place the shallots, garlic, chillies, cumin, turmeric, lemongrass and galangal and process to a smooth paste, adding a little water if necessary to keep the blades turning. Combine the paste and the oxtail and set aside to marinate for 2 hours.

Bring 3 litres (105 fl oz/12 cups) water to the boil in a large saucepan. Add the marinated oxtail and all the remaining ingredients. Return to the boil, uncovered, and simmer over low heat for 2–3 hours or until the oxtail is tender and the sauce has thickened. Skim all the fat off the top and check the seasoning.

Place the oxtail and sauce in a bowl and serve with steamed rice.

NOTES: A quick way of removing seeds from long dried chillies is to snip the ends with scissors and poke a long skewer down the middle to release them, then simply upturn and empty the seeds from the chilli. The oxtail can be replaced with beef chuck steak or lamb shoulder. You could even try skinless chicken thigh fillets instead – boil the broth for an hour until it thickens then add the chicken and cook till tender.

The scallops can, of course, be replaced with most types of seafood. You can also add whatever vegetables you like. If using prawns or firm white fish, you can remove the oyster sauce and replace it with hot bean paste.

STIR-FRIED SEA SCALLOPS & BEANS WITH OYSTER SAUCE

SERVES 4, OR 8 AS PART OF A SHARED ASIAN BANQUET

80 ml (2½ fl oz/⅓ cup) peanut oil

16 large sea scallops

100 g (3½ oz) green beans, topped and tailed, cut into 8 cm (3¼ inch) lengths

2 spring onions (scallions), cut into 8 cm (3¼ inch) lengths, green and white part

3 cm (1¼ inch) piece fresh ginger, peeled and finely chopped

8 garlic cloves, finely chopped

1 tablespoon Shaoxing rice wine or dry sherry

1 tablespoon yellow bean soy sauce (available from Asian grocers)

1 tablespoon Chinkiang black vinegar

1 teaspoon sugar

3 tablespoons oyster sauce

3 tablespoons chicken stock

freshly ground white pepper

1 fresh long red chilli, seeded and julienned

1 small handful coriander (cilantro) leaves

Heat a wok over high heat until smoking.

Add half the oil and, when hot, quickly stir-fry the scallops in batches until almost cooked through. Remove and wipe the wok clean with paper towel.

Reheat the wok with another tablespoon of oil and stir-fry the beans and spring onions until just tender, then remove from the wok.

Heat the last tablespoon of oil in the wok and stir-fry the ginger and garlic until fragrant.

Deglaze the wok with the Shaoxing, then add the soy sauce, vinegar, sugar, oyster sauce and stock and simmer for 2 minutes. Return the cooked scallops, beans and spring onions to the wok and toss together.

Spoon into a serving bowl, give it a good grind of white pepper and sprinkle with the chilli strips and coriander leaves.

I'm a fan of the red bean curd as it has an interesting taste. If you're not big on it then leave it out and add some sweet bean paste or the hot variety that contains puréed chillies instead.

STIR-FRIED MUSSELS WITH RED BEAN CURD & CHILLIES

SERVES 4, OR 8 AS PART OF A SHARED ASIAN BANQUET

500 g (1 lb 2 oz) mussels
2 teaspoons fermented red bean curd
    (available from Asian grocers)
1 tablespoon yellow bean soy sauce
    (available from Asian grocers)
3 tablespoons chicken stock
½ teaspoon sugar
2 tablespoons vegetable oil
4 garlic cloves, finely chopped
3 small wild green (bird's eye) chillies,
    thinly sliced
2 tablespoons Shaoxing rice wine or
    dry sherry
1 small red capsicum (pepper), seeded
    and diced
2 spring onions (scallions), shredded,
    including some green tops

Wash the mussels in cold water, debearding if necessary and discard any that are broken or don't close when tapped on the work surface.

Mash the red bean curd with a fork then stir in the yellow bean soy sauce, stock and sugar.

Heat a wok until just smoking. Add the oil and, when hot, add the garlic and chillies and stir-fry until fragrant. Deglaze the wok with the Shaoxing, then add the mussels and stir-fry for 2–3 minutes. Add the capsicum and bean sauce mixture and toss together.

Cover the wok with a lid or a round metal tray and cook for 2–3 minutes, shaking the wok occasionally, or until the shells just begin to open. Use a slotted spoon to transfer the mussels to a bowl, discarding any unopened mussels.

Return the wok to the heat and simmer the sauce, uncovered, until it reduces and thickens slightly. Pour the sauce over the mussels and sprinkle with the shredded spring onion to serve.

NOTE: This is another dish that works well with scallops, prawns or cubes of firm white-fleshed fish.

I love the simplicity of this fish recipe. I use prosciutto instead of Yunnan ham as it is easier to get. Any large firm white-fleshed fish works well. Try to get the bamboo shoots that are in large pieces, not thinly sliced, and wash them very well.

STEAMED SNAPPER WITH SHIITAKE, PROSCIUTTO & BAMBOO

SERVES 4, OR 8 AS PART OF A SHARED ASIAN BANQUET

400 g (14 oz) snapper fillet, skin off
1 tablespoon peanut oil
4 thin prosciutto slices, each piece
    halved to match the shape of the fish
80 g (2¾ oz) tinned whole bamboo
    shoots, julienned
4 dried shiitake mushrooms, soaked in
    warm water for 30 minutes, stalks
    removed, julienned
2 spring onions (scallions), julienned
freshly ground white pepper

SEASONING
2 tablespoons light soy sauce
3 tablespoons chicken stock
½ teaspoon sugar
1 tablespoon peanut oil
¼ teaspoon sesame oil
½ teaspoon sea salt

Cut the snapper fillet into eight equal portions.

Mix all the seasoning ingredients together.

Brush the peanut oil all over two round plates, each large enough to hold four pieces of fish. Alternatively, lay a piece of baking paper on the base of both baskets of a double steamer, with the paper big enough to come a little up the sides so the liquid won't run off. Place the fish on the plates or paper, allowing space between each piece. Layer the prosciutto, bamboo shoots and mushrooms over the top of each piece. Pour the seasoning over. If using plates, place in a steamer basket.

Place the steamer baskets over a saucepan or wok of rapidly boiling water, cover and steam for 5–6 minutes or until the fish is just cooked through. You may want to swap the steamer baskets around after 3 minutes. Carefully remove the plates or paper from the steamer and sprinkle with spring onion and a pinch of white pepper.

NOTE: A few slices of chilli and ginger make a welcome addition to this dish; just sprinkle over at the stage where you put the fish in the steamer.

There are a lot of ingredients here but it is a cinch to put together. You can use any type of noodle – mung bean or fresh egg noodles work just as well as rice noddles.

STIR-FRIED RICE NOODLES WITH CHICKEN & OCTOPUS

SERVES 4, OR 8 AS PART OF A SHARED ASIAN BANQUET

125 ml (4 fl oz/½ cup) vegetable oil

3 skinless chicken thigh fillets, sliced

1 teaspoon finely chopped garlic

1 egg, lightly whisked

300 g (10½ oz) fresh rice noodles

2 tablespoons light soy sauce

80 ml (2½ fl oz/⅓ cup) dark soy sauce

125 ml (4 fl oz/½ cup) chicken stock

50 g (1¾ oz) cleaned baby octopus, sliced

2 pieces Chinese mustard greens (available from Asian grocers), julienned

handful bean sprouts

½ teaspoon powdered white pepper

1 teaspoon sesame oil

35 g (1¼ oz/¼ cup) roasted peanuts

2 spring onions (scallions), cut into fine rounds, including a little of the green

Heat a wok over high heat until just smoking and add 3 tablespoons of the vegetable oil. Add the chicken and stir-fry for 3–4 minutes or until almost cooked. Remove the chicken from the wok and place in a bowl.

Wipe the wok out with paper towel, place it back on the heat and add the rest of the vegetable oil. When hot, add the garlic and stir-fry for a few seconds. Add the egg and cook until it just starts to set, then add the noodles and stir well. Add the soy sauces and stock and bring to the boil.

Return the chicken to the wok and add the octopus. Cook over very high heat for 1 minute or until the octopus is cooked. Add the mustard greens, bean sprouts, white pepper and sesame oil, cook for 1 minute then transfer to a serving dish. Serve with the peanuts and spring onion on the side, or sprinkled over the dish.

NOTE: Try adding pork, prawn or crab meat along with the chicken for added interest.

This is a cross between boiled and fried rice. The rice takes on great flavour and you can add any favourites to the dish such as dried shrimp, bacon, bamboo shoots or water chestnuts.

CLAY POT CHICKEN RICE

SERVES 4, OR 6–8 AS PART OF A SHARED ASIAN BANQUET

400 g (14 oz/2 cups) long-grain rice,
    washed
600 ml (21 fl oz) chicken stock
4 skinless chicken thigh fillets, cut into
    small dice
1 Chinese sausage (lap cheong), sliced
6 dried black shiitake mushrooms,
    soaked, simmered until cooked,
    then quartered
4 cm (1½ inch) piece fresh ginger,
    julienned
1 spring onion (scallion), green and
    white part, julienned

MARINADE
2 tablespoons vegetable oil
½ teaspoon sesame oil
3 teaspoons oyster sauce
2 teaspoons light soy sauce
3 teaspoons dark soy sauce
1 tablespoon Shaoxing rice wine or
    dry sherry
1 tablespoon sugar
½ teaspoon white pepper
1 tablespoon cornflour (cornstarch)

Soak a small clay pot in water for 24 hours before using for the first time.

Put the rice and stock in the clay pot, cover and cook over low heat with a heat diffuser if you have one for 20 minutes.

Meanwhile, mix together all the marinade ingredients and pour over the chicken, mixing well.

Spread the marinated chicken, Chinese sausage, mushrooms and ginger on top of the rice. Cover and cook for a further 10 minutes.

Mix everything through the rice, sprinkle with the spring onions and serve.

NOTE: I like to mix in a beaten egg when I'm folding all the ingredients through the rice at the end. It gives the dish a luscious texture that I adore.

The classic sweet and sour is so tasty. You can replace the pork with chicken or fish. The sauce alone is great poured over whole fried crisp fish.

SWEET & SOUR PORK

SERVES 4, OR 6–8 AS PART OF A SHARED ASIAN BANQUET

300 g (10½ oz) pork loin, cubed

1½ tablespoons Shaoxing rice wine
   or dry sherry

½ teaspoon sea salt

2 eggs, organic, if possible, lightly
   whisked

35 g (1¼ oz/¼ cup) plain (all-purpose)
   flour, plus extra for dusting

500 ml (17 fl oz/2 cups) vegetable oil,
   for deep-frying, plus extra

2 teaspoons finely chopped fresh ginger

3 spring onions (scallions), cut into 4 cm
   (1½ inch) lengths

½ red capsicum (pepper), cut into
   large dice

½ green capsicum (pepper), cut into
   large dice

125 ml (4 fl oz/½ cup) chicken stock

2 tablespoons light soy sauce

4 tablespoons sugar

80 ml (2½ fl oz/⅓ cup) Chinese red
   vinegar (available from Asian grocers)

2 tablespoons tomato sauce (ketchup)

50 g (1¾ oz/⅓ cup) roughly chopped
   fresh pineapple

½ teaspoon sesame oil

1 small handful coriander (cilantro)
   leaves

Combine the pork, ½ tablespoon of the Shaoxing and the sea salt in a bowl and set aside to marinate for 30 minutes.

Beat the egg and flour with about 2 tablespoons water to form a light batter.

Heat the oil in a wok or deep-fryer over high heat until just smoking (180°C/350°F, or a cube of bread dropped into the oil turns golden brown in 15 seconds). Dust the pork lightly in flour then dip the pork in the batter and carefully deep-fry the slices in batches until golden. Drain on paper towel. Pour the oil from the wok and wipe the wok clean with paper towel.

Heat the wok again, with 2 tablespoons of vegetable oil, until just smoking and stir-fry the ginger, onion and capsicum until fragrant. Deglaze the wok with the remaining Shaoxing then add the stock, soy sauce, sugar, vinegar and tomato sauce. Bring to the boil, reduce the heat and simmer until slightly thickened.

Add the pineapple and pork and cook for 30 seconds more. Transfer to a serving dish and sprinkle with the sesame oil and scatter over the coriander leaves.

NOTE: If you want the sauce a bit thicker use a little cornflour mixed in water – add it bit by bit so you don't thicken it too much. If you are in a major rush tinned pineapple is acceptable.

This is lovely with a fried egg on top and chilli sauce for a simple meal. Fried rice goes with any stir-fry, curry or Asian salad.

FRAGRANT FRIED RICE

SERVES 4, OR 8 AS PART OF A SHARED ASIAN BANQUET

2 tablespoons vegetable oil

½ red onion, thinly sliced

2 long spring onions (scallions), cut into 4 cm (1½ inch) lengths

2 fresh long red chillies, seeded and sliced

2 teaspoons finely chopped fresh ginger

2 garlic cloves, finely chopped

400 g (14 oz) cooked long-grain white rice, cold

30 ml (1 fl oz) Shaoxing rice wine or dry sherry

50 ml (1½ fl oz) yellow bean soy sauce

30 g (1 oz) caster (superfine) sugar

Heat a wok or large non-stick frying pan over high heat until hot. Add the oil and when it is very hot, add the onion and spring onion and stir-fry for 1 minute. Add the chilli and stir-fry for 30 seconds. Add the ginger and garlic and stir-fry for 30 seconds. Add the rice and stir-fry, mixing thoroughly and breaking up any clumps of rice. Add the Shaoxing, soy sauce and sugar. Continue to stir-fry until the seasoning is totally combined and the rice has no clumps. Serve.

NOTE: For best results use day-old rice, as freshly cooked rice tends to be too moist.

I also use this curry as a base for a stir-fry. Just add the paste, palm sugar and fish sauce after stir-frying your meat or fish and you have an amazingly flavoured dish.

GREEN CURRY OF PRAWNS

SERVES 4, OR 8 AS PART OF A SHARED ASIAN BANQUET

250 ml (9 fl oz/1 cup) coconut cream
3 tablespoons vegetable oil
6 kaffir lime leaves
80 ml (2½ fl oz/⅓ cup) fish sauce
1 tablespoon grated palm sugar (jaggery)
500 ml (17 fl oz/2 cups) coconut milk
8 raw large king prawns (shrimp), peeled and deveined
4 wild green (bird's eye) chillies, lightly crushed
3 fresh long red chillies, halved lengthways and seeded
10 Thai pea eggplants (aubergines)
5 apple eggplants (aubergines), quartered
12 sweet Thai basil leaves

GREEN CURRY PASTE
5 coriander seeds
5 cumin seeds
5 white peppercorns
6 wild green (bird's eye) chillies, chopped
3 fresh long green chillies, seeded and chopped
2 lemongrass stems, pale part only, tough outer leaves removed, chopped
2 tablespoons chopped fresh galangal
10 red Asian shallots, chopped
5 garlic cloves, chopped
3 coriander (cilantro) roots, scraped and chopped
1 tablespoon chopped fresh turmeric
finely grated zest of 1 kaffir lime
1 teaspoon Thai shrimp paste, wrapped in foil and roasted until fragrant

For the green curry paste, lightly roast the coriander and cumin seeds and the peppercorns in a dry heavy-based frying pan, then grind to a powder in a coffee or spice grinder. Pound the chillies, lemongrass, galangal, shallots, garlic, coriander roots, turmeric, lime zest and shrimp paste in a mortar with a pestle.

Pass all the ground and pounded ingredients through a mincer twice, or use a blender to process until smooth, adding a little water or oil if necessary. You can also just keep pounding with the pestle to produce a fine paste. Set aside 130 g (4¾ oz/about ½ cup) of paste for the curry. (Any leftover paste will freeze until next time.)

To make the curry, place the coconut cream and oil in a heavy-based frying pan over high heat and bring to the boil, stirring continuously. When the coconut cream splits (the oil and solids separate), add the curry paste. Crush the lime leaves in your hand, add them to the pan and fry for 10–15 minutes or until the mixture is sizzling and aromatic (use your nose).

Add the fish sauce and cook for 1 minute. Add the palm sugar and coconut milk and bring to the boil. Add the prawns, chillies and eggplants and simmer gently for 4 minutes or until the prawns are just cooked and the pea and apple eggplants are still a little crunchy. Stir in the basil just before serving.

You could use skinless chicken breast fillets in this dish; however, I find that the thighs are less likely to overcook. I have done this with sliced pork loin and it works well too. A nice firm white-fleshed fish such as blue-eye trevalla has its place with these seasonings if you feel like a healthier option.

STEAMED LEMON CHICKEN

SERVES 4, OR 8 AS PART OF A SHARED ASIAN BANQUET

350 g (12 oz) free-range or organic
    chicken thigh fillets, skin on, each
    cut into 3 pieces
1½ lemons, quartered lengthways
pinch of freshly ground white pepper,
    to serve
2 spring onions (scallions), julienned,
    to serve
steamed rice, to serve
Asian greens, to serve

MARINADE
1 tablespoon Shaoxing rice wine or
    dry sherry
1½ tablespoons light soy sauce
1½ tablespoons oyster sauce
2 teaspoons sesame oil
1 tablespoon peanut oil
2 teaspoons sea salt
1 tablespoon sugar

Place the chicken in a shallow non-metallic heatproof bowl, squeeze the juice from the lemons over the top, then add the lemon skins to the bowl as well. Add all the marinade ingredients to the bowl. Mix thoroughly and set aside for 30 minutes.

Cover the bowl tightly with foil and place in a large bamboo steamer over a saucepan or wok of rapidly boiling water. Place the lid on and steam the chicken for 25 minutes, removing (and replacing) the lid and foil to turn the chicken once during this time, or until cooked through.

Turn off the heat and carefully remove the bowl from the steamer. Remove the foil, sprinkle with the pepper and spring onions to serve.

Serve with steamed rice and Asian greens.

ICEBERG LETTUCE & MUSHROOM SALAD

SERVES 4, OR 6–8 AS PART OF A SHARED ASIAN BANQUET

1 large wedge iceberg lettuce, washed
and dried
2 tablespoons peanut oil
200 g (7 oz) assorted mushrooms, such
as enoki, shiitake, shimeji and oyster,
torn into even-sized pieces
1 red onion, halved and thinly sliced
1 handful combined mint and coriander
(cilantro) leaves
1 spring onion (scallion), julienned
2 French shallots, peeled, finely sliced
and deep-fried until golden
1 teaspoon ground roast rice (see note)

DRESSING
1 garlic clove, roughly chopped
3 coriander (cilantro) roots, scraped and
chopped
2 small wild green (bird's eye) chillies,
roughly chopped
pinch of sea salt
pinch of caster (superfine) sugar
3 tablespoons lime juice
2 tablespoons fish sauce

For the dressing, pound the garlic and coriander roots in a mortar with a pestle until quite fine, then add the chillies and pound a little further. Add the salt and sugar to form a paste. Add the lime juice and fish sauce and taste to balance, adjusting if necessary.

Shred the iceberg lettuce and place on a plate.

Heat a wok over high heat until smoking. Add the oil and, when hot, stir-fry the mushrooms and onion for 30–60 seconds or until just starting to soften. Remove from the heat. Add the dressing, herbs and spring onion and toss together. Spoon the mixture over the lettuce. Sprinkle the salad with the fried brown shallots and ground roast rice to serve.

NOTE: To make ground roast rice, place a thin layer of uncooked jasmine rice in a frying pan over low heat or in a 150°C (300°F/Gas 2) oven and toast until it becomes opaque but not coloured. When cool, grind finely in a mortar with a pestle.

A little sliced or chopped pickled ginger is also great mixed into the honey soy sauce. There is enough sauce so you can serve rice with this dish and pour the sauce over the rice. This is one of those dishes that is very hard to stop eating.

SESAME PRAWN CUTLETS WITH A HONEY SOY DIPPING SAUCE

SERVES 4, OR 8 AS PART OF A SHARED ASIAN BANQUET

12 raw king prawns (shrimp), peeled, deveined and tail intact
120 g (4¼ oz/2 cups) Japanese breadcrumbs (panko)
3 tablespoons sesame seeds
sea salt
150 g (5½ oz/1 cup) plain (all-purpose) flour
2 eggs, organic, if possible, lightly whisked
vegetable oil, for deep-frying

HONEY SOY DIPPING SAUCE
175 g (6 oz/½ cup) honey
2 tablespoons soy sauce
4 cm (1½ inch) piece fresh ginger, peeled, finely grated
½ fresh long red chilli, seeded and finely diced
3 teaspoons fresh lime juice
sea salt and freshly ground black pepper

For the sauce, combine 170 ml (5½ fl oz/⅔ cup) water, the honey, soy sauce, ginger and chilli in a small saucepan over medium heat. Bring to the boil and simmer, stirring constantly, for 2–3 minutes or until the sauce is slightly thickened. Remove from the heat and stir in the lime juice. Check seasoning.

Use a small sharp knife to cut a slit along the back of each prawn (don't cut all the way). Use your fingers to gently open each prawn to sit flat. Keep the tail intact.

Combine the panko crumbs and sesame seeds in a bowl and season to taste with salt.

Place the flour and egg in separate bowls. Dip a few prawns at a time into the flour until well coated, shaking off any excess. Dip into the egg and then the panko mixture, pressing firmly to coat. Place the prawns in a single layer on a plate.

Add enough oil to a large frying pan to reach a depth of 2 cm (¾ inch). Heat over medium heat. Cook the prawns in batches without crowding the pan for 1–2 minutes or until just cooked through and golden. Drain on paper towel.

Repeat with the remaining prawns. If necessary, add some extra oil to the frying pan, and bring back up to temperature before cooking the next batch of prawns. Serve the prawns on a platter with the honey soy dipping sauce on the side.

NOTE: You can use ordinary breadcrumbs, but the panko are more of a statement and have a great crunch.

What I like most about this dish, besides my love of cashew nuts in Chinese cooking, is the fact that it is essentially a dry stir-fry. It's a nice change not to be too saucy. You can substitute the trevalla for other seafood, or for chicken.

SPICY STIR-FRIED BLUE-EYE TREVALLA WITH CASHEWS

SERVES 2, OR 4 AS PART OF A SHARED ASIAN BANQUET

350 g (12 oz) blue-eye trevalla, cut into
    3 cm (1¼ inch) dice
1 tablespoon vegetable oil
4 cm (1½ inch) piece fresh ginger, peeled
    and thinly sliced
4 celery stalks, diagonally sliced
4 spring onions (scallions), cut into 4 cm
    (1½ inch) batons
2 fresh long red chillies, cut into 1 cm
    (½ inch) rounds
40 g (1½ oz/¼ cup) cashew nuts,
    roasted
3 tablespoons chicken stock
steamed rice, to serve

MARINADE
1½ teaspoons Shaoxing rice wine or
    dry sherry
1 teaspoon vegetable oil
1½ teaspoons light soy sauce
1 teaspoon finely chopped fresh ginger
1 teaspoon sea salt
1 teaspoon sugar

For the marinade, mix together the Shaoxing, oil, soy sauce, ginger, sea salt and sugar.

Add the blue-eye trevalla and leave to marinate for 20 minutes.

Heat a wok over high heat until just smoking. Add the oil and, when hot, add the ginger and stir-fry for 10 seconds or until fragrant. Add the fish with its marinade, spreading it evenly around the wok. Cook undisturbed for 1 minute, allowing the fish to start to brown, then stir-fry until the fish is lightly browned all over.

Add the celery, spring onion, chilli and cashews and stir-fry for 1 minute. Swirl in the stock and continue to stir-fry until the fish is just cooked through and the sauce is slightly thickened. Transfer to a plate and serve with steamed rice.

NOTE: I like it hot so I don't seed the chillies, but if you want colour without too much heat then seeding them is the way to go. Replace the cashew nuts with peanuts if that takes your fancy.

MEDITERRANEAN SHARED TABLES

Although these dishes work well together on a shared table, you can also pick some as entrées and others as mains. Extra virgin olive oil, sea salt, freshly ground pepper and lemon all mix well with fresh herbs and tomatoes to give these recipes their wonderful flavours.

I love this dish served with roasted new potatoes. The marinade can also be used on all types of poultry, or brush it over potatoes before roasting. You could also combine the marinade with butter and stuff it under the skin of a chicken, or brush it over a lamb leg or shoulder before baking.

MEDITERRANEAN SPATCHCOCK

SERVES 4

4 x 500 g (1lb 2 oz) fresh spatchcocks
150 ml (5 fl oz) olive oil, for frying
1 lemon, quartered, to serve
extra virgin olive oil (optional), to serve

MARINADE
1 tablespoon finely grated lemon zest
3 garlic cloves, finely chopped
2 tablespoons thyme leaves, finely
    chopped
2 tablespoons rosemary leaves, finely
    chopped
2 teaspoons ground turmeric
3 teaspoons ground coriander
1 tablespoon lemon juice
100 ml (31/2 fl oz) olive oil
sea salt and freshly ground black pepper

For the marinade, combine all the ingredients apart from the oil in a mortar and pound with a pestle to a paste. Stir in the oil and season to taste.

Place the spatchcock on a chopping board and use poultry shears or strong kitchen scissors to cut along both sides of the backbone and discard it. Open out the spatchcock, place skin side up on the board and push down on the breastbone to flatten. Repeat with the other three spatchcocks. Place the spatchcocks in a large bowl and pour over the marinade. Toss to coat well and refrigerate for 6 hours.

Preheat the oven to 170°C (325°F/Gas 3).

Heat the oil in a large frying pan over medium–high heat. Seal the spatchcocks on all sides, then place on a baking tray and bake for 10–15 minutes or until cooked through. Remove and rest for 5 minutes. To serve, place a spatchcock on each of four plates, drizzle with a little extra virgin olive oil, if desired, sprinkle with sea salt, give a good grind of pepper and serve with a lemon quarter on the side.

This dish is perfect with scallops or diced blue-eye trevalla, and artichokes or fennel are great substitutes for the shiitakes. Use whatever mushroom variety takes your fancy: I like soft oyster mushrooms, too.

FRESH SHIITAKE MUSHROOMS SAUTEED WITH PRAWNS & WHITE POLENTA

SERVES 4

125 ml (4 fl oz/½ cup) extra virgin olive oil

500 g (1 lb 2 oz) fresh shiitake mushrooms, stems removed and caps roughly diced

8 raw large king prawns (shrimp), peeled, deveined and roughly chopped

1 garlic clove, finely chopped

½ lemon

sea salt and freshly ground black pepper

POLENTA

200 g (7 oz) white polenta (cornmeal)

60 g (2¼ oz/½ cup) grated fontina cheese

6 tablespoons freshly grated parmesan cheese

100 g (3½ oz) unsalted butter

For the polenta, fill a large saucepan with 600 ml (21 fl oz) water, add a good pinch of sea salt and bring to the boil over high heat. Add the polenta and cook, stirring constantly with a whisk, for 2 minutes.

Reduce the heat to low and cook, stirring occasionally with a wooden spoon, for 50 minutes or until smooth. Stir in the fontina, parmesan and butter. Remove from the heat and keep warm.

For the mushrooms, heat the olive oil in a frying pan over medium–high heat and cook the mushrooms until tender. Add the chopped prawns and garlic and cook for 1 minute or until the prawn meat is just cooked through. Season to taste with lemon juice, salt and pepper.

To serve, spoon the warm polenta onto serving plates and top with the mushrooms and prawns.

NOTE: You can use yellow polenta or whatever type you like but I prefer the delicate flavour of white.

Any cheese is great here – feta, Burrata or a dollop of fresh ricotta all work nicely. Use fresh mozzarella, not the type you grate onto pizza. If it's the height of summer and green, red and yellow capsicums are available, cook one of each to add wonderful colour.

BUFFALO MOZZARELLA, CAPSICUM & ONION SALAD

SERVES 4

8 small pickling onions, skin on
100 ml (3½ fl oz) extra virgin olive oil, plus extra
2 large red capsicums (peppers)
2 tablespoons balsamic vinegar
sea salt and freshly ground black pepper
4 small balls fresh buffalo mozzarella cheese
½ bunch basil, small leaves only

Place the onions in a deep frying pan or a shallow saucepan that will hold them in one layer, and pour enough oil in the pan to come halfway up the onions. Turn the heat to low and fry the onions gently until they are very tender. Carefully peel the onions.

Preheat a barbecue to high. Rub the capsicums with oil and place them on the barbecue. Cook the capsicums, turning them regularly, until they are well blackened on all sides. Place the capsicums in a bowl, cover with plastic wrap and leave to steam for about 30 minutes. Peel the capsicums, remove the seeds and slice into thin strips about 1–1.5 cm (½–⅝ inch) thick. Dress the capsicum with the remaining oil, and the balsamic, salt and pepper.

Cut each mozzarella ball into wedges and arrange on a large serving platter or divide among four plates. Add the dressed capsicum, the onions and the basil. Drizzle with the remaining oil and add another grind of pepper.

These fritters can also be served with aïoli. Salt cod can be poached in a tomato and chilli sauce and turned into a delicious sauce for soft polenta, or as a topping for bruschetta. Don't forget to soak the salt cod first.

SALT COD FRITTERS WITH FRESH LEMON

MAKES ABOUT 34 FRITTERS

250 g (9 oz) salt cod

250 g (9 oz) all-purpose potatoes (such as desiree), quartered

125 ml (4 fl oz/½ cup) milk

80 ml (2½ fl oz/⅓ cup) extra virgin olive oil

4 garlic cloves, finely chopped

3 spring onions (scallions), finely chopped

1 egg yolk

freshly ground black pepper

TO CRUMB

150 g (5½ oz/1 cup) plain (all-purpose) flour

2 eggs, organic, if possible, lightly whisked with 1 tablespoon water

120 g (4¼ oz/2 cups) Japanese breadcrumbs (panko)

1 litre (35 fl oz/4 cups) vegetable oil, for deep-frying

2 lemons, cut into wedges

Place the salt cod in a bowl and cover with cold water. Cover the bowl with plastic wrap, place in the fridge and soak for 24 hours, changing the water several times. Drain the fish and dry well, then remove the skin and bones and discard. Place the flesh in a large saucepan, cover with water, bring to the boil and gently simmer, covered, for about 20 minutes. Drain and set aside.

Steam the potatoes until just cooked.

Combine the milk and 1 tablespoon of the olive oil in a small saucepan and heat until warm.

In a heavy-based saucepan, heat the remaining olive oil over low heat. Add the garlic and spring onion and fry for 1–2 minutes, then add the salt cod and stir well with a wooden spoon to break up the flesh.

Put the potatoes through a mouli grater or ricer and add to the pan, beating well to make a paste. Gradually beat in the warm milk and oil mixture, then add the egg yolk and pepper to taste. Remove from the heat, cool and chill. Check the seasoning and adjust if necessary.

Roll level tablespoons of the mixture into balls. In small batches, dust with the flour, coat with the egg mixture, then coat with the panko crumbs and shake away any excess.

Add the vegetable oil to a deep pot and heat the oil to 180°C (350°F) (a cube of bread dropped in the oil will turn golden brown in 15 seconds when it reaches this temperature). Deep-fry the salt cod fritters for about 1 minute or until golden and crisp. Drain on paper towel.

Drizzle with a squeeze of lemon and serve immediately.

Add depth of flavour and a touch of Spain with some good-quality chopped smoked bacon thrown in with the garlic and chillies.

SPAGHETTI WITH MUSSELS, PRAWNS & CHILLI

SERVES 4

1 kg (2 lb 4 oz) large black mussels
3 tablespoons dry white wine
3 tablespoons extra virgin olive oil
8 raw king prawns (shrimp), peeled and deveined
3 garlic cloves, minced
2 small dried red chillies, crumbled
1 handful flat-leaf (Italian) parsley, roughly chopped, plus extra
sea salt and freshly ground black pepper
400 g (14 oz) good-quality dried spaghetti

Wash the mussels in cold water, debearding if necessary and discard any that are broken or don't close when tapped on the work surface.

Place the wine in a saucepan over medium–high heat and add the mussels. Cover and steam the mussels in the wine for 4–5 minutes until they open then remove the opened mussels from the pan. Discard any mussels that haven't opened. Strain and reserve the mussel juice.

Add half of the oil to the pan. When hot, add the prawns and sear quickly on all sides to colour. Remove the prawns from the pan and set aside. Add the garlic and chilli and cook for 2 minutes or until opaque, then add the mussels, strained liquid, parsley and the remaining oil. Return the prawns to the pan and check seasoning. The liquid from the mussels may be salty enough; if not, add a little salt and some pepper.

Meanwhile cook the spaghetti in a saucepan of boiling salted water for 8 minutes or until *al dente*. Drain and mix through the mussel and prawn sauce. Spoon the sauce and pasta into four pasta bowls and serve immediately, sprinkled with extra chopped parsley.

NOTE: *You could also serve this sauce with penne or soft polenta.*

Any firm white-fleshed fish is good in this recipe, plus the sauce is also a great partner to chicken. For some extras on the side, serve with boiled and seasoned green beans or broccoli and roast potatoes.

ROASTED SNAPPER FILLETS WITH LEEKS, GREEN OLIVES & BREADCRUMBS

SERVES 4

extra virgin olive oil

2 leeks, white part only, trimmed, washed and cut into 5 mm (¼ inch) rounds

sea salt and freshly ground black pepper

4 garlic cloves, crushed

8 large green olives, pitted and roughly chopped

1 tablespoon baby capers, rinsed and chopped

1 tablespoon flat-leaf (Italian) parsley, finely chopped

1 lemon

4 x 200 g (7 oz) snapper fillets, skin off

30 g (1 oz/½ cup) coarse fresh breadcrumbs, toasted

Preheat the oven to 200°C (400°F/Gas 6).

Place a little oil in a non-stick frying pan over low heat. Add the leek, season with salt and cook gently for 20 minutes. Add the garlic and cook for 5 minutes, then add the olives, capers and parsley and toss through. Drizzle with a little more oil and the juice of half the lemon and season with pepper. Set aside and keep warm (it can be reheated when the fish is ready to be served).

Place the fish in a roasting tin, drizzle with oil and sprinkle with salt. Roast in the oven for 8 minutes or until the fish is just cooked through.

Place a spoonful of the leek mixture in the middle of each of four plates, and top with a fish fillet, a little more of the leek mixture and a squeeze of lemon.

Finish with a drizzle of oil and a sprinkle of the breadcrumbs. Season with salt and pepper.

NOTE: Place a straightened paperclip or cake tester into the fish to check whether it is cooked – the fish should still have resistance when you remove it from the oven. If it is perfectly cooked in the oven it will be overcooked by the time it gets to the table. Black olives and roasted cherry tomatoes are nice additions.

This gnocchi is easy to make and goes brilliantly with the fresh tomato sauce (opposite). If you want to make extra, it keeps well in the freezer.

FRESH GNOCCHI

SERVES 4

1 kg (2 lb 4 oz) sebago potatoes
2 bay leaves (either fresh or dried)
small handful salt, plus 1 teaspoon extra
200 g (7 oz/1⅓ cups) plain (all-purpose) flour
1 egg, beaten
3 tablespoons extra virgin olive oil

Place the potatoes in a saucepan and cover with cold water. Add the bay leaves and salt and simmer over medium heat until cooked through.

Strain, then peel and mouli the potatoes. Turn out onto a clean work surface and form a well in the middle.

Gently incorporate the flour, the extra salt, egg and oil until the dough is uniform and even. Knead gently for 30 seconds. The dough should be soft, but still hold its shape. It should have an even consistency with no cracks. If the dough is sticking to your hand, add a little more flour.

Cut the dough into five pieces and, using your hands, roll each piece into a long roll about 1.5–2 cm (⅝–¾ inch) thick. Cut the rolls with a knife into pieces 3 cm (1¼ inches) long.

Cook in boiling salted water until the gnocchi float to the surface (about 2–3 minutes) and serve with your favourite sauce.

NOTE: Uncooked gnocchi will keep in the fridge for a day or if you have made extra it can be stored in the freezer in an airtight container for two months.

Prosciutto works as well as pancetta and it's a swap I love to do. It's fun making your own gnocchi. There are heaps of recipes to choose from but the key to them all is not to overwork the dough.

PAN-FRIED GNOCCHI WITH TOMATO & BASIL SAUCE & CRISPY PANCETTA

SERVES 4

400 g (14 oz) fresh gnocchi (see opposite)
olive oil, for frying
100 g (3½ oz) thinly sliced pancetta
¼ bunch basil, leaves only, to serve
freshly ground black pepper
freshly grated parmesan cheese, to serve

TOMATO AND BASIL SAUCE

1.5 kg (3 lb 5 oz) very ripe vine-ripened tomatoes
100 ml (3½ fl oz) extra virgin olive oil
2 tablespoons red wine vinegar
½ bunch basil, leaves only, plus a small handful, leaves finely chopped, extra
2 tablespoons finely chopped thyme
2 garlic cloves, finely chopped
1 heaped teaspoon caster (superfine) sugar
sea salt and freshly ground black pepper

Preheat the oven to 150°C (300°F/Gas 2).

For the tomato and basil sauce, use a small sharp knife to remove the cores and lightly score the bases of the tomatoes. Place the tomatoes in a large baking dish, base side up, and drizzle with the oil, vinegar, basil and thyme. Roast the tomatoes, uncovered, for 1½ hours or until they are very soft and the skin is peeling away. Cool slightly. Remove and discard the skins. Roughly chop the flesh and place in a medium heavy-based saucepan with any leftover juices, as well as the garlic and sugar. Season to taste and simmer, uncovered, over medium–low heat for about 30 minutes, stirring frequently, or until the sauce has thickened. Stir through the chopped basil and check the seasoning.

Meanwhile, bring a large saucepan of salted water to the boil. Add the gnocchi and bring to a simmer. Once cooked and floating, remove the gnocchi with a slotted spoon and drain well.

In a large non-stick frying pan, heat some oil. Pan-fry the gnocchi until golden brown, being careful not to break them. Remove from the pan and set aside.

To the same pan add a splash of oil and fry the pancetta until crisp and golden. Drain on paper towel and set aside.

Divide the gnocchi between four bowls, top with the tomato and basil sauce, crispy pancetta, basil leaves, a drizzle of oil, pepper and parmesan.

NOTE: The tomato and basil sauce can be served with crumbed veal or chicken. Or you could sear 6 skinless chicken thigh fillets until browned and place in an ovenproof dish. Pour over the tomato and basil sauce and top with freshly grated mozzarella and parmesan. Bake in the oven for about 10 minutes or until just cooked. Serve with a green salad.

Any firm white-fleshed fish is wonderful with a herb crust. Not only does it give great flavour to the fish but more importantly it keeps it moist during cooking.

ROAST OCEAN TROUT WITH A HERB CRUST

SERVES 4

2 tablespoons extra virgin olive oil
½ brown onion, finely diced
2 garlic cloves, finely diced
60 g (2¼ oz/1 cup) toasted coarse
    breadcrumbs
2 tablespoons chopped fresh ginger
1 teaspoon coriander seeds, roasted
    and roughly pounded
3 tablespoons chopped coriander
    (cilantro) leaves
3 tablespoons chopped flat-leaf (Italian)
    parsley leaves
3 tablespoons chopped chives
1 tablespoon grated lemon zest (no pith)
sea salt and freshly ground pepper
90 g (3¼ oz) unsalted butter, softened
4 x 180 g (6 oz) ocean trout fillet, skin off
lemon wedges, to serve

Preheat the oven to 200°C (400°F/Gas 6).

For the herb crust, heat the oil in a frying pan over medium heat. Add the onion and garlic and sweat for 5 minutes or until soft. Remove from the pan and transfer to a stainless steel bowl. Add the breadcrumbs, ginger, coriander seeds and leaves, parsley, chives, lemon zest, sea salt and a good grind of pepper. Mix thoroughly, add the butter and mix again; it should start to come together.

On a chopping board, squash the crust mixture into a square that is slightly larger than the fish fillet. Lay the fish, presentation side down, on the crust mixture and cut the fish and its coating into four pieces. Slide a fish slice under the first piece, carefully turn the fish and its coating over and put in a roasting tin, crust side up. Repeat with the remaining portions. Cook in the oven for 6–7 minutes or until cooked to your liking. (The time will differ depending on the thickness of the fillets.)

Carefully place one fish portion on each of four plates and squeeze over fresh lemon juice. Serve immediately.

NOTE: Fennel or zucchini soup makes a wonderful sauce for this fish. Add a salad and a few boiled and buttered baby spuds and you have a fantastic meal. You can make a cracking sauce for fish by roasting tomatoes in the oven until very soft, removing the skin and then boiling with a couple of tablespoons of good red wine vinegar and chopped flat-leaf (Italian) parsley.

The salsa is great with seafood and works well with chicken, pork, lamb or beef. It also works beautifully as part of a vegetable antipasto table. The fish doesn't have to be grilled – it could be pan-fried, poached or roasted.

BARBECUED BARRAMUNDI WITH ROAST CAPSICUM & OLIVE SALSA

SERVES 4

4 x 200 g (7 oz) barramundi fillets, skin on
sea salt and freshly ground pepper
extra virgin olive oil
1 lemon, cut into quarters

SALSA
3 yellow capsicums (peppers)
3 red capsicums (peppers)
80 ml (2½ fl oz/⅓ cup) extra virgin olive oil, plus extra
sea salt and freshly ground pepper
2 small red onions, finely diced
3 garlic cloves, finely chopped
3 anchovy fillets, chopped
40 g (1½ oz/¼ cup) pitted kalamata or whole Ligurian olives
1 tablespoon salted capers, rinsed
2 tablespoons flat-leaf (Italian) parsley leaves, finely chopped
splash of red wine vinegar

Preheat the oven to 180°C (350°F/Gas 4).

For the salsa, cut the capsicums in half and remove the seeds. Toss with 2 tablespoons of the oil to coat and salt and pepper to taste. Arrange the capsicums, cut side down, on two baking trays and roast for 35–40 minutes or until the skins blister. Transfer to a bowl and cover with plastic wrap. When cool enough to handle, peel the capsicums and cut into large dice.

Meanwhile, in a non-stick frying pan, heat 2 tablespoons of oil over low heat. Add the onion, garlic and a sprinkle of salt. Cook for 30–40 minutes or until the onion is meltingly tender. Add the anchovies, olives and capers and toss them through the onion mix. Remove from the heat. Add the parsley and capsicum, and drizzle with the extra olive oil and the vinegar. Check seasoning and finish with a grind of pepper. Set the salsa aside.

Preheat a barbecue grill to high. Season the fish fillets and brush with a little extra oil. Grill the fish, skin side down, for 2 minutes, then turn over and cook for a further 2 minutes or until done to your liking. If the fillets are thick, this could take as long as 10 minutes. Serve the fish with the salsa and lemon wedges.

NOTE: It is important to place the capsicums in a bowl and cover with plastic wrap. This keeps the cooking process going and softens them, adding to the intensity of the flavour because they are steamed with their own heat.

The chicken skin is so tasty. Fat is flavour so balance your diet by eating plenty of vegetables and fish as well. I like this dish because boiling the vegetables first makes it fast and simple. Serve with potatoes, or purée of yams and a green salad.

CHICKEN WITH PANCETTA, FENNEL & CELERIAC

SERVES 4

extra virgin olive oil

4 free-range chicken breasts, winglet attached and skin on

sea salt and freshly ground pepper

80 g (2¾ oz) pancetta, cut into lardons

6 baby fennel heads, quartered and boiled until tender

1 small celeriac, peeled, cut into quarters and boiled until tender

1 red onion, quartered and boiled until tender

40 g (1½ oz) butter

3 tablespoons good-quality red wine vinegar

Heat a non-stick frying pan large enough to hold all the chicken over medium heat. Add a splash of oil. Season the chicken with salt and place skin side down in the pan. Cook for about 5–6 minutes, then turn over carefully and cook for a further 5 minutes.

Remove the chicken from the pan and rest it in a warm place while you finish the vegetables.

Add a little more oil to the pan with the remaining ingredients except the butter and vinegar. Turn the heat up and cook the vegetables, stirring constantly, until they start to brown and heat through. Add the butter and vinegar and remove from the heat. Swirl the pan until the butter makes a sauce, add pepper and check the seasoning.

Divide the vegetables among plates and place a chicken breast on top of each. Drizzle with extra virgin olive oil, a pinch more seasoning and serve.

This dish is a cracker with chicken or quail instead of the duck.
I also like it with raisins in place of the olives.

HONEY-BRAISED DUCK WITH ALMONDS & OLIVES

SERVES 4

4 large duck legs
sea salt and freshly ground black pepper
2 tablespoons extra virgin olive oil
8 brown shallots, halved lengthways
    if large
500 ml (17 fl oz/2 cups) chicken stock
1 tablespoon honey
½ teaspoon ground cinnamon
½ teaspoon ground coriander
6 garlic cloves
1 rosemary sprig, leaves picked
100 g (3½ oz) whole blanched almonds
180 g (6 oz) green olives
juice of 1 lemon

Preheat the oven to 200°C (400°F/Gas 6).

Cut the duck legs in two at the joint and season with salt and pepper.

Heat the oil over medium heat in a deep, ovenproof, heavy-based frying pan until it smokes. Add the duck, skin side down, and brown for 2 minutes on each side. Remove from the pan and set aside.

Add the shallots to the pan and toss over medium heat until golden, then remove and set aside.

Discard the oil and rendered duck fat. Add the stock, stirring to loosen any caramelised bits from the bottom of the pan. Stir in the honey and spices, return the duck to the pan, skin side up, along with the shallots, garlic, rosemary, almonds and olives and season. Bring to the boil.

Transfer the pan to the oven and bake for 10 minutes. Reduce the temperature to 180°C (350°F/Gas 4), cover with a tight-fitting lid or several layers of foil and bake for a further 40 minutes.

Strain the duck mixture through a fine sieve into a large bowl, reserving the solids. Return the liquid to the pan and simmer, uncovered, to reduce by about half or until a good sauce consistency. Skim any impurities from the top. Add the lemon juice. Return the duck and other solids to the pan, heat through and taste for seasoning.

Serve with a bowl of steamed couscous or rice and a large salad.

I love to serve this ragout in the middle of the table as part of a shared feast for the family. Add polenta, a green salad and whatever seasonal vegetables are begging to be boiled and served with olive oil and lemon juice. Don't forget bread for mopping up the juices.

ITALIAN-STYLE LAMB RAGOUT

SERVES 8

1.5 kg (3 lb 5 oz) good-quality lamb
    shoulder, cut into 3 cm (1¼ inch) dice

MARINADE
6 fresh bay leaves
1 teaspoon juniper berries
½ teaspoon black peppercorns
2 fresh sprigs rosemary
6 garlic cloves, finely chopped
500 ml (17 fl oz/2 cups) cabernet
    sauvignon

BRAISE
185 ml (6 fl oz/¾ cup) olive oil
1 brown onion, finely chopped
3 garlic cloves, crushed
2½ tablespoons tomato paste
    (concentrated purée)
1 tablespoon plain (all-purpose) flour
750 ml (26 fl oz/3 cups) chicken stock,
    plus a little extra if necessary
250 ml (9 fl oz/1 cup) tomato passata
    (puréed tomatoes)
sea salt and freshly ground black pepper
2 carrots, roughly chopped
2 celery stalks, roughly chopped

Combine the diced lamb with the marinade of bay leaves, juniper berries, peppercorns, rosemary, garlic and wine. Marinate in the fridge for 8 hours.

Remove the lamb from the marinade, pass the liquid through a fine sieve and reserve. Discard the other ingredients.

Heat 2 tablespoons of the oil in a deep heavy-based saucepan over high heat. Seal the marinated lamb in batches until browned all over. Remove the meat from the pan and set aside.

Add the remaining oil and reduce the heat to low. Cook the onion and garlic until softened. Add the tomato paste and cook for a few minutes, then add the flour and cook, stirring constantly, for 3 minutes. Slowly whisk in 250 ml (9 fl oz/1 cup) of the reserved marinade liquid, stirring constantly for a few minutes until there are no lumps. Stir through the stock and passata and season well with salt and pepper. Return the lamb and any juices to the pan, along with the carrot and celery. There should be enough liquid to cover (add a little more stock to cover if necessary).

Cover and cook for 45–60 minutes or until the meat is tender and sauce has reduced. Check seasoning and adjust if necessary.

NOTE: This braise can be of any meat you like – beef, veal, pork, rabbit or goat. Simply adjust the cooking time accordingly. I like to serve with mashed potato or soft polenta, or as a pasta sauce with penne – finish with grated Reggiano.

Instead of the baking tray, you could cook the mushrooms in an attractive casserole dish and it can go straight to the table.

THYME-ROASTED MUSHROOMS

SERVES 6–8 AS A SIDE DISH

1 kg (2 lb 4 oz) large Swiss brown
    mushrooms
20 g (¾ oz) butter, melted
1½ tablespoons extra virgin olive oil
good pinch of thyme leaves
sea salt and freshly ground black pepper

Preheat the oven to 200°C (400°F/Gas 6).

Place the mushrooms, stems up, on a large baking tray. Brush with the butter and drizzle with the oil. Scatter with the thyme leaves and season with salt and pepper. Roast in the oven for approximately 15 minutes or until tender.

Serve the mushrooms with a green salad with a citrusy dressing, or on toast.

These involtini can be served with soft creamy polenta – use plenty of butter and add blanched green beans. Thin slices of swordfish can be used instead of the veal to make this delicious dish.

SICILIAN VEAL INVOLTINI WITH HERBED RISONI, ROAST TOMATO & OREGANO SAUCE

SERVES 4

35 g (1¼ oz/⅓ cup) freshly grated pecorino cheese
1 tablespoon fresh breadcrumbs
1 tablespoon finely chopped flat-leaf (Italian) parsley
1½ tablespoons toasted pine nuts
1 heaped tablespoon dried currants, soaked in warm water
    for 1 hour, then drained
pinch of rosemary leaves, finely chopped
pinch of sea salt
pinch of freshly ground white pepper
4 x 150 g (5½ oz) veal escalopes
2 tablespoons olive oil

HERBED RISONI
400 g (14 oz/2 cups) risoni
80 ml (2½ fl oz/⅓ cup) extra virgin olive oil
8 large basil leaves
1 garlic clove
finely grated zest of ½ lemon, no pith
sea salt and freshly ground black pepper

ROAST TOMATO AND OREGANO SAUCE
10 very ripe, vine-ripened tomatoes
65 ml (2¼ fl oz) good-quality extra virgin olive oil
2 tablespoons good-quality red wine vinegar
¼ bunch oregano, leaves picked and chopped
2 thyme sprigs, leaves picked and chopped
sea salt and freshly ground black pepper
2 teaspoons chopped oregano, extra
½ teaspoon chopped thyme, extra
½ teaspoon caster (superfine) sugar

Preheat the oven to 180°C (350°F/Gas 4).

In a bowl stir together the pecorino, breadcrumbs, parsley, pine nuts, drained currants, rosemary and seasoning until well mixed.

Lay the pieces of veal out on a work surface and spread the breadcrumb mixture over each piece, spreading it out thinly and evenly. Roll up each piece tightly, starting from a short side, and secure with toothpicks.

Heat the oil in a heavy-based frying pan over medium heat and cook the involtini in batches until sealed all over. Remove from the heat, place on a tray lined with baking paper and bake for 3–5 minutes or until cooked through. Once the involtini has rested, remove and discard the toothpicks.

HERBED RISONI

Cook the risoni in a saucepan of boiling salted water, stirring frequently, until *al dente*.

Meanwhile, in a food processor or with a stick blender, blend the oil, basil leaves, garlic and lemon zest.

Drain the risoni well and toss through the herbed oil. Season with salt and pepper.

ROAST TOMATO AND OREGANO SAUCE

Preheat the oven to 150°C (300°F/Gas 2).

Use a small sharp knife to remove the cores and lightly score the bases of the tomatoes.

Place the tomatoes in a large ovenproof dish, base side up, and drizzle with the combined oil, vinegar, oregano, thyme and a good sprinkle of salt and pepper. Roast the tomatoes, uncovered, for 1¼ hours or until the tomatoes are very soft and the skin is peeling away. Cool slightly, and remove and discard the tomato skins.

Place the peeled tomatoes with the pan juices in a medium heavy-based suacepan. Simmer, uncovered, stirring often, over medium heat for about 1 hour. Stir in the extra herbs and the sugar. Simmer for a further 30 minutes until the sauce has reduced and slightly thickened. Check seasoning.

To serve, divide the risoni among four plates or large pasta-style bowls. Place an involtini on each and top with the roast tomato and oregano sauce.

NOTE: The roast tomato and oregano sauce can be tossed through any cooked pasta and finished with grated pecorino, or used in lasagne. You can make the sauce ahead of time.

MEXICAN FEASTS

I have, over the last few years, fallen in love with Mexican food. I love the spice and complexity, and most of all I love to wrap just about anything in a tortilla. Place some meat, a bit of chicken or grilled fish, guacamole and a little shaved cabbage salad in the middle of the table, heat the tortillas and let the magic happen.

So simple, just roast a chicken and fold through. This sauce also works with any other roasted meat you might like to try.

ROAST CHICKEN IN GREEN SALSA

SERVES 4

500 g (1 lb 2 oz) tinned tomatillos,
    drained
2 fresh jalapeño chillies, seeded and
    finely chopped
3 small garlic cloves
1 teaspoon ground cumin
sea salt
25 g (1 oz/½ cup) chopped coriander
    (cilantro) leaves
1 roast chicken, flesh and skin removed
    from the bone, cut into chunks
fresh or fried tortillas (optional), to serve

For the salsa, place the tomatillos and jalapeño chillies in a saucepan with enough water to cover and bring just to the boil. Lower the heat and simmer gently, turning the tomatillos and chillies occasionally for 15–20 minutes or until the tomatillos are tender but haven't started falling apart.

Drain the tomatillos and chillies in a colander. Put the tomatillos, chillies, garlic, cumin and a good pinch of salt in a blender or food processor and pulse just until the tomatillos are coarsely chopped. Add the coriander and blend until smooth.

Return the sauce to the pan over medium heat and fold the chicken through to gently reheat. Place in a bowl and serve with fresh or fried tortillas if desired.

NOTE: A cabbage salad works beautifully with any of the following Mexican dishes. All that's required is a little shaved cabbage, peeled, seeded and sliced cucumber, sliced spring or Spanish onion, combined with lots of coriander leaves and a chopped jalapeño, seasoned with sea salt and freshly ground pepper and dressed with lime juice and extra virgin olive oil. Perfect. You can also serve this dish wrapped in a tortilla.

Too easy – this sauce is great with any fresh tacos. You can also just fry the tomatoes and when they start to melt, add a spoonful of chipotle chilli powder, cook for a minute longer, remove from the heat and squeeze in fresh lime. Cabbage salad, guacamole, sour cream, tortillas and a margarita ... heaven.

SOFT TACOS WITH SMOKY SHREDDED PORK

SERVES 8–12

800 g (1 lb 12 oz) boneless pork shoulder
4 garlic cloves, roughly chopped
1 brown onion, quartered
sea salt
2 tablespoons olive oil
255 g (9 oz/1½ cups) raisins
16 corn tortillas
guacamole, to serve
sour cream, to serve

ROASTED TOMATO
CHIPOTLE SAUCE
4 garlic cloves, unpeeled
9 roma (plum) tomatoes
3 chipotle chillies in adobo sauce
1 tablespoon olive oil
sea salt

Place the pork in a medium saucepan with the garlic and onion. Add a good pinch of salt, cover with water and bring to a simmer. Cook, covered, for about 2 hours on medium–low heat or until the pork is tender. Allow to cool before shredding the meat with your hands.

Preheat the oven grill (broiler).

For the roasted tomato chipotle sauce, heat a heavy-based saucepan over high heat and add the unpeeled garlic. Roast for 15 minutes, turning halfway through, until the outsides are blackened. Remove from the heat, squeeze the garlic flesh out of the skins and roughly chop.

Place the whole tomatoes under the grill and cook until the skins are dark and blistered on all sides. Remove from the grill and allow to cool slightly before peeling.

Place the tomatoes and garlic in a food processor and blend. Add the chillies one at a time and process to combine. Taste the sauce as you go and, depending on the heat level you prefer, add more.

Heat the oil in a non-stick saucepan and cook the sauce over medium heat, stirring frequently, until the sauce has slightly thickened. Season to taste.

Heat 2 tablespoons of olive oil in a heavy-based saucepan, add the shredded pork and cook until it is crispy and golden. Add the raisins and roasted tomato chipotle sauce and cook for 5–6 minutes or until the mixture has thickened.

To serve, microwave the tortillas for 10–20 seconds, or according to the packet instructions, to soften and warm through. Place a large spoonful of the pork in each tortilla and top with the salsa, guacamole and a generous dollop of sour cream.

NOTE: Marinate and grill fish or chicken to add more elements to your feast. The tortillas can also be steamed or warmed in a frying pan.

These two salsas work perfectly as starters with corn chips; they both go beautifully with grilled fish and they are essential in the middle of the table with all the other Mexican recipes that follow with tortillas, to make fresh tacos.

GUACAMOLE & MEXICAN SALSA WITH CORN CHIPS

SERVES 8–12

SALSA
5 roma (plum) tomatoes, seeded and
    finely diced
1 small red onion, finely diced
½ bunch coriander (cilantro), finely
    chopped
small handful mint leaves, finely chopped
30 ml (1 fl oz) fresh lemon juice
sea salt and freshly ground black pepper

GUACAMOLE
½ small red onion
3 fresh jalapeño chillies, halved
    lengthways and seeded
½ bunch coriander (cilantro), leaves only
sea salt and freshly ground black pepper
3 ripe avocados
juice of 2 limes
8 cherry tomatoes, roughly chopped

corn chips, to serve

To make the salsa, combine all the ingredients in a bowl and season to taste.

To make the guacamole, finely chop the onion, chillies and coriander leaves. Place in a mortar with a generous amount of sea salt and pound with a pestle until you have a rough paste.

Halve the avocados, remove the stone and skin and add to the mortar, pounding with the pestle until they start to mash.

Add the lime juice and a good grind of pepper and fold through. Add the cherry tomatoes and fold through gently.

Serve the salsa in one bowl and the guacamole in another surrounded by the corn chips.

Like many of the other Mexican recipes featured in this section, these are great with all the meats to make a fresh taco, or served first with corn chips. I also love the beans with a fried, boiled or poached egg on top. Breakfast taco, anyone?

CHILLI BLACK BEANS WITH JALAPENO SALSA

SERVES 6–8

CHILLI BLACK BEANS

2 teaspoons olive oil

1 brown onion, finely chopped

2 garlic cloves, finely chopped

150 g (5½ oz) speck or pancetta,
  finely chopped

3 fresh long red chillies, finely chopped

1 teaspoon sweet paprika

large pinch of cayenne pepper

400 g (14 oz) tinned chopped tomatoes

2 teaspoons brown sugar

15 g (½ oz/¼ cup) finely chopped
  coriander (cilantro) root

400 g (14 oz) tinned black beans, rinsed
  and drained

sea salt and freshly ground black pepper

JALAPENO SALSA

60 g (2¼ oz/¼ cup) sliced pickled
  jalapeños

3 tablespoons pickled jalapeño brine

small handful coriander (cilantro) leaves

2 spring onions (scallions), roughly
  chopped

soft tortillas, to serve

Preheat the oven to 220°C (425°F/Gas 7).

Heat the oil in a large non-stick frying pan over high heat. Add the onion, garlic and speck or pancetta and cook for 5 minutes or until the onion is soft. Add the chilli, paprika and cayenne pepper and cook for a further 2 minutes.

Add the tomatoes, sugar, coriander root, black beans, salt and pepper, reduce the heat to medium and cook for 10 minutes or until slightly thickened. Set aside and keep warm.

For the salsa, place the jalapeño, brine, coriander and spring onion in a food processor and process until roughly chopped. Set aside.

Serve the salsa with the warm chilli black beans and soft tortillas.

This twice cooked pork dish is amazing. You can serve it a bit chunky after it comes out of the oven or you can shred it. I also like to fry it rather than roast it once it has had its first cook.

CARNITAS (BRAISED & FRIED PORK)

SERVES 8–12

1 kg (2 lb 4 oz) fatty pork shoulder,
    cut into 4 cm (1½ inch) dice
½ orange, halved
2 bay leaves
1 white onion, thinly sliced
3 tablespoons vegetable oil
5 garlic cloves
1 tablespoon sweetened condensed milk
1 teaspoon dried oregano
sea salt, to taste
fresh tortillas, to serve
guacamole, to serve
sour cream, to serve
cabbage and onion salad, to serve

Place all the ingredients and 500 ml (17 fl oz/2 cups) water in a wide heavy-based saucepan and bring to the boil. Reduce the heat and simmer, uncovered, skimming the surface regularly, for 1½ hours or until tender.

Preheat the oven to 220°C (425°F/Gas 7).

Place the pork and fat in an ovenproof dish and roast, uncovered, in the oven for 20 minutes or until browned.

Transfer to a serving plate or bowl and serve with the tortillas, guacamole, sour cream and salad.

These ribs are a great centre piece for fresh tortillas. The meat falls off the bone. Build a great fresh taco by adding cabbage salad, sour cream and guacamole. Like the meatballs, it also makes a great stand-alone meat dish with potatoes or rice, or for that matter soft polenta; I know, a bit cross-cultural but very tasty!

MEXICAN-STYLE BRAISED BEEF SHORT RIBS

SERVES 8–12

1 kg (2 lb 4 oz) beef short ribs

2 tablespoons olive oil

1 fresh long green chilli, seeded, finely chopped

3 garlic cloves, finely chopped

large pinch of sea salt

freshly ground white pepper

1 teaspoon ground cumin

½ teaspoon ground chilli powder

1 teaspoon ground coriander

½ teaspoon ground allspice

400 g (14 oz) tinned chopped tomatoes

1½ tablespoons chopped pickled jalapeño chillies

1 tablespoon brown sugar

1 tablespoon red wine vinegar

600 ml (21 fl oz) chicken stock

juice of 1 lime

1 bunch coriander (cilantro), leaves picked and roughly chopped, to serve

Place the ribs in a heavy-based saucepan, cover with cold water and bring to the boil. Strain, return to the saucepan and cover again with fresh water. Bring to the boil and simmer for 1 hour. Turn off the heat and allow the ribs to cool in the water. Drain, place in a bowl and set aside.

Preheat the oven to 180°C (350°F/Gas 4).

Heat the oil in a wide heavy-based saucepan over low heat and sauté the green chilli, garlic, salt, pepper, cumin, chilli powder, ground coriander and allspice for 1 minute or until fragrant. Add the tomatoes, jalapeños, sugar, vinegar and stock and bring to a simmer. Pour this mixture over the ribs, toss to coat, and place on a baking tray lined with baking paper, in a wide saucepan or a frying pan. Pour over any remaining marinade.

Roast the ribs for 1¾–2 hours, stirring occasionally, or until the meat is golden and falling from the bones. Drain off the excess fat. Gently stir through the lime juice, garnish with coriander and serve.

Love these, look Italian, could only be Mexican when you taste them. The chipotle in adobo sauce is awesome to have around the kitchen. Add to any sauce for a fantastic smoky lift and I love them chopped through a vinaigrette for a salad. Serve these with tortillas for a fresh taco or serve them with rice or potatoes for a hearty tasty meal. If you really want to have a fab lunch, make a sandwich out of them. So damn good!

MEATBALLS IN CHIPOTLE SAUCE

MAKES ABOUT 18 MEATBALLS

300 g (10½ oz) minced (ground) beef
300 g (10½ oz) minced (ground) pork
½ teaspoon ground cumin
1 garlic clove, finely chopped
sea salt and freshly ground black pepper
60 g (2¼ oz/1 cup) fresh breadcrumbs
2 large eggs, organic, if possible
1 tablespoon milk
extra virgin olive oil
Manchego or pecorino cheese, to serve

SAUCE
4 ripe tomatoes
6 chipotle chillies in adobo sauce
   (see note)
2 garlic cloves
¼ teaspoon ground cumin
½ teaspoon dried oregano
½ teaspoon sea salt
250 ml (9 fl oz/1 cup) chicken stock

For the chipotle sauce, place the tomatoes, chillies and their sauce, garlic, cumin, oregano and salt in a blender. Add the stock and process until quite smooth.

For the meatballs, place the beef, pork, cumin, garlic, 1 teaspoon salt and a grind of pepper in a bowl. Mix well, then stir in the breadcrumbs, eggs and milk. To check the seasoning, cook a small amount of mixture and taste it. Form the mince mixture into small walnut-sized balls.

Heat a large frying pan with a splash of olive oil over medium heat. Add the meatballs and brown gently for 2 minutes. Add the sauce and cook gently for 6 minutes, stirring occasionally, or until the sauce starts to thicken. Reduce the heat to medium–low and cook, uncovered, until the sauce reduces to about half its original volume and coats the meatballs.

To serve, spoon the meatballs onto a serving plate and grate a little Manchego or pecorino over the top.

NOTE: Chipotle chillies are red jalapeños that have been smoked and dried. Adobo sauce is typically flavoured with spices such as paprika, bay leaves and oregano. The two are available together in tins at selected delis and Mexican food suppliers.

SWEET THINGS

These are lovely, delicious, simple sweets that will have you cooking like a pro in no time. My one tip is to buy scales and measure everything. You can't fail if you do.

The passionfruit butter is seriously good. Spread it on toast with a cup of tea for breakfast.

MELTING MOMENTS WITH PASSIONFRUIT BUTTER

MAKES 13 FILLED BISCUITS

250 g (9 oz) unsalted butter, softened
    and diced
75 g (2½ oz) icing (confectioners') sugar
1 lemon, zest finely grated
250 g (9 oz/1⅔ cups) plain (all-purpose)
    flour
50 g (1¾ oz) rice flour
butter, for greasing
icing (confectioners') sugar, to dust

PASSIONFRUIT BUTTER
30 g (1 oz) unsalted butter, softened
100 g (3½ oz) icing (confectioners')
    sugar
2 tablespoons passionfruit pulp (about
    1 passionfruit)

Preheat the oven to 180°C (350°/Gas 4).

Use electric beaters to beat the butter, icing sugar and lemon zest until pale and creamy. Use a wooden spoon to stir in the flours until combined. Knead the mixture gently on a lightly floured work surface until smooth, then cover in plastic wrap and rest for 30 minutes in the fridge.

Divide the mixture into 26 pieces and roll into balls. Place on a greased baking tray and flatten the balls with the back of a fork. Bake for 12–16 minutes or until crisp and light golden. Stand for 5 minutes then transfer to a cooling rack.

For the passionfruit butter, beat the butter with a wooden spoon until pale and creamy. Add half the icing sugar and beat until well combined. Add the passionfruit pulp and the remaining icing sugar and beat until well combined and fluffy.

Use a palette knife or piping (icing) bag with a 1 cm (½ inch) nozzle to spread the passionfruit butter onto half the cooled biscuits. Top with the remaining biscuits and dust with icing sugar.

This tart a bit of a classic — a crowd-pleaser and an excellent dinner party dessert.
It is also terrific with yoghurt or yoghurt ice cream.

MOROCCAN ORANGE TART WITH MASCARPONE

SERVES 10–12

oil spray, for greasing

1 sheet good-quality sweet shortcrust
   pastry (bought or homemade),
   enough to line a 24 cm (9½ inch)
   flan (tart) tin (see below)

egg wash, for glazing

2 eggs, organic, if possible

75 g (2½ oz) caster (superfine) sugar

90 ml (3 fl oz) thin (pouring) cream,
   whisked to soft peaks

110 g (3¾ oz) almond meal

30 ml (1 fl oz) fresh lemon juice

1 orange, finely zested, no white pith

2 tablespoons fresh orange juice

mascarpone cheese, to serve

SWEET SHORTCRUST PASTRY

250 g (9 oz/1⅔ cups) plain (all-purpose)
   flour

75 g (2½ oz) unsalted butter, diced

pinch of sea salt

90 g (3¼ oz) icing (confectioners') sugar,
   sifted

55 ml (1¾ fl oz) full-cream milk

2 egg yolks

For the sweet shortcrust pastry, place the flour, butter, salt and icing sugar in a food processor and process for 20 seconds. Add the milk and the egg yolks and process for 30 seconds or until a mass forms. Turn out onto a lightly floured work surface and knead lightly for a few moments then flatten the pasty and form a ball. Wrap in plastic wrap and place in the fridge for 1 hour.

Preheat the oven to 180°C (350°/Gas 4). Spray a 24 cm (9½ inch) loose-based fluted flan (tart) tin with oil.

Lightly flour a work surface and roll out the pastry 2 cm (¾ inch) wider than the tart tin.

Roll the pastry over the rolling pin and gently ease it into the tin, pushing the pastry in gently so it follows the fluting. Place in the fridge and rest for 30 minutes.

Prick the pastry base a few times with a fork to prevent blistering and rising. Line the tart case with baking paper and uncooked rice and blind bake for 20 minutes. Remove the paper and rice, brush the pastry shell with the egg wash and bake for a further 10 minutes.

For the filling, use electric beaters to beat the eggs and sugar until thick, creamy and the mixture holds a trail. Use a wooden spoon to fold in the whisked cream and remaining ingredients except for the mascarpone, until combined and smooth.

Spoon the mixture into the prepared pastry case and bake at 180°C (350°/Gas 4) for 25–30 minutes or until puffed and golden and firm to touch. Allow to cool before cutting.

Serve the tart in slices with a spoonful of mascarpone.

NOTE: Sweet shortcrust pastry is simple to make and worth the small effort, but feel free to buy a good-quality pastry frozen from the supermarket as it is quite a handy item to have in the freezer, and you can simply use sheets as you need them.

I love these little biscuits served with zabaglione or crumbled over rich vanilla ice cream.

ALMOND BISCUITS

MAKES 32

100 g (3½ oz) unsalted butter

115 g (4 oz/⅓ cup) golden syrup (golden treacle)

115 g (4 oz) caster (superfine) sugar

115 g (4 oz) plain (all-purpose) flour, sifted

1 teaspoon fresh lemon juice

125 g (4½ oz) flaked almonds

Preheat the oven to 160°C (315°F/Gas 2–3).

Line two baking trays with baking paper.

Put the butter, golden syrup and sugar in a saucepan over low heat and stir until dissolved. Do not let the mixture boil. Remove from the heat and stir in the flour, lemon juice and almonds. Put well-spaced teaspoonfuls of the mixture on the baking trays.

Place in the oven for 10 minutes or until bubbling and golden.

Remove from the oven and leave on the trays to cool.

Store in an airtight container in single layers with baking paper between each.

You need a sugar thermometer to make the nougat but they are cheap and very handy if you like baking. The higher the temperature of the sugar, the harder the nougat sets.

ITALIAN NOUGAT

MAKES ABOUT 48 PIECES

60 g (2¼ oz) whole blanched almonds

440 g (15½ oz/2 cups) caster (superfine) sugar

250 ml (9 fl oz/1 cup) liquid glucose

175 g (6 oz/½ cup) honey

¼ teaspoon salt

2 egg whites

1 teaspoon natural vanilla extract

125 g (4½ oz) unsalted butter, roughly chopped

oil, for greasing

Preheat the oven to 180°C (350°/Gas 4).

Place the almonds on a baking tray and bake for 5 minutes or until golden. Set aside to cool.

Put the sugar, liquid glucose, honey, salt and 3 tablespoons water in a saucepan over low heat and stir until the sugar dissolves. Bring to the boil and cook on a fast simmer until the temperature reaches 122°C (252°F) on a sugar thermometer and a small amount of the syrup forms a hard ball when dropped in cold water. This should take about 8 minutes.

Use electric beaters to whisk the egg whites until firm peaks form. Pour one-quarter of the hot syrup in a thin stream over the egg whites, beating constantly. Continue beating for 3–5 minutes or until the mixture is thick enough to hold its shape.

Cook the remaining syrup to 157°C (315°F), about 5 minutes, or until a small amount of syrup forms brittle threads when dropped in cold water. Pour the remainder of the hot syrup over the meringue in a thin stream, beating constantly until the mixture is very thick. Add the vanilla and butter and beat for 5 minutes or until thick again.

Use a wooden spoon to stir in the cooled toasted almonds. Turn the mixture into a greased 28 x 18 cm (11¼ x 7 inch) lamington tin and smooth the top with a spatula. Refrigerate until firm.

Loosen the edges of the nougat all around then turn out in a large block. Use a sharp knife to cut the nougat into 4 x 2.5 cm (1½ x 1 inch) pieces.

Wrap each piece individually in cellulose paper or waxed baking paper. Keep in the fridge.

Key lime pie is a classic American dessert. I love the zing of the lime with the sweetness of the cream.

KEY LIME PIE

SERVES 6–8

butter, for greasing
1 sheet good-quality sweet shortcrust
    pastry (bought or homemade),
    enough to line a 24 cm (9½ inch)
    flan (tart) tin (see page 195)
300 ml (10½ fl oz) thin (pouring) cream

FILLING
125 ml (4 fl oz/½ cup) fresh lime juice
2 x 4 g (⅛ oz) gelatine sheets
    (titanium strength)
3 egg yolks
400 g (14 oz) tin sweetened condensed
    milk
1½ teaspoons lime zest

Preheat the oven to 180°C (350°F/Gas 4).

Lightly grease a loose-based 24 cm (9½ inch) flan (tart) tin.

Roll out the pastry on a lightly floured work surface to 5 mm (¼ inch) thick. Line the flan tin with the pastry and trim the edges. Cover and refrigerate for 30 minutes. It is important to rest the shell or it will shrink.

Prick the base a few times with a fork to prevent blistering and rising. Line the tart case with baking paper and uncooked rice and blind bake for 12 minutes, then remove the paper and rice and bake for a further 5 minutes to dry and colour. Leave to cool before adding the filling.

For the filling, warm the lime juice in a small saucepan. Soak the gelatine in water to soften, squeeze out the excess water and add to the lime juice and stir until dissolved. Use electric beaters on high speed to beat the egg yolks and condensed milk together in a medium bowl until pale and thick. Add the lime juice mixture and the lime zest to the egg yolks, beating to combine. Pour the filling into the prepared pie shell. Refrigerate for 3 hours or until set.

Whip the cream in a small bowl until soft peaks form. To serve, spoon the cream over the pie.

NOTE: Another serving idea is to spoon the lime filling into glass dishes. When set, top with the whipped cream and serve with sponge fingers. It's easier than making pastry but you would need to change the name to 'key lime'.

For a quirky dessert, cut the cake into small cubes and arrange in martini glasses with a good drizzle of the passionfruit syrup and a generous spoonful of the mango salsa.

PASSIONFRUIT SYRUP CAKE WITH MANGO SALSA

SERVES 10–12

PASSIONFRUIT SYRUP
350 ml (12 fl oz) passionfruit purée
150 g (5½ oz/⅔ cup) caster (superfine) sugar

PASSIONFRUIT SYRUP CAKE
150 g (5½ oz) unsalted butter, softened
220 g (7¾ oz/1 cup) caster (superfine) sugar
1 teaspoon natural vanilla extract
4 eggs, organic, if possible
275 g (9¾ oz) Greek-style yoghurt
300 g (10½ oz/2 cups) self-raising flour, sifted

MANGO SALSA
3 large mangoes, peeled, flesh removed from stone and cut into large dice
2 tablespoons elderflower cordial
juice of 1 lemon
1 small handful mint leaves, finely chopped

Preheat the oven to 160°C (315°F/Gas 2–3).

For the passionfruit syrup, put the passionfruit purée, 200 ml (7 fl oz) water and the sugar in a small saucepan over medium heat and stir until the sugar has dissolved. Bring to the boil, reduce the heat to low and cook for 10–15 minutes or until syrupy. Keep warm.

For the cake, use electric beaters to beat the butter and sugar for 10–15 minutes or until pale and creamy. Add the vanilla, then the eggs one at a time, beating well after each addition. Add the yoghurt and beat until combined. Fold through the flour.

Spoon the mixture into a 22 cm (8½ inch) round spring-form cake tin lined with baking paper and bake for 50 minutes or until a skewer inserted into the centre of the cake comes out clean.

For the mango salsa, place all the ingredients in a bowl and toss to combine.

Remove the cake from the tin and place on a serving plate. Pierce the cake evenly with a metal skewer, then drizzle generously with the warm passionfruit syrup. Top with the mango salsa and extra passionfruit syrup if desired.

NOTE: If mangoes aren't about, try ripe stone fruit instead.

Whatever berries or stone fruit are in season are great to use in this cake.
It is also nice finished with whipped cream instead of yoghurt.

STRAWBERRY & YOGHURT CAKE

SERVES 12–16

200 g (7 oz) polenta (cornmeal)
200 g (7 oz/1⅓ cups) self-raising flour
1 teaspoon baking powder
275 g (9¾ oz/1¼ cups) caster (superfine)
   sugar
110 g (3¾ oz) unsalted butter, melted
600 g (1 lb 5 oz) plain yoghurt
200 ml (7 fl oz) warm water
600 g (1 lb 5 oz/4 cups) strawberries,
   hulled and chopped
icing (confectioners') sugar, for dusting

Preheat the oven to 170°C (325°F/Gas 3).

Line and grease a 22 cm (8½ inch) cake tin. Place the dry ingredients in a large mixing bowl. Stir to combine and make a well in the centre. Add the butter, 300 g (10½ oz) of the yoghurt and the water and beat with a wooden spoon until well blended. Stir through half of the strawberries and pour into the tin.

Bake for 2 hours or until a skewer inserted into the centre comes out clean.

Place on a cooling rack and stand for 15 minutes before removing from the tin.

Once completely cool, top the cake with the remaining yoghurt and strawberries. To serve, dust with icing sugar.

NOTE: I like to use a square tin for this one, to mix it up. Plus it makes it easy to portion and this is a cake that lasts well for a couple of days – hold off adding the yoghurt and strawberries until just before serving.

This cake is a cracker. Use any fruit in season. Leave out the chocolate in the cream filling and use vanilla and sugar for a richer flavour. You can also leave out the cocoa in the meringue if you like.

BLUEBERRY, RASPBERRY & STRAWBERRY ROULADE CAKE

SERVES 6

butter, for greasing

ROULADE
6 egg whites
275 g (9¾ oz/1¼ cups) caster (superfine) sugar
1 tablespoon cornflour (cornstarch)
1 teaspoon fresh lemon juice
2 tablespoons icing (confectioners') sugar
2 tablespoons unsweetened cocoa powder

FILLING
250 g (9 oz/1 cup) thick (double) cream
1 punnet each of blueberries, raspberries and strawberries
2–3 tablespoons coarsely grated dark chocolate

For the roulade, preheat the oven to 170°C (325°F/Gas 3). Line a Swiss roll (jelly roll) tin with baking paper. Butter the paper.

Use an electric mixer fitted with a whisk attachment to whisk the egg whites on high speed until soft peaks form. Gradually add half the caster sugar then beat in the remaining caster sugar until stiff, glossy peaks form. Fold in the cornflour and lemon juice.

Spread the meringue evenly in the prepared tin. Bake for 20 minutes or until pale golden, then allow to cool for 1 hour.

Place a sheet of baking paper on a work surface and dust with the icing sugar and cocoa powder, reserving some for later. Turn the meringue onto the baking paper. Carefully remove the top sheet of paper.

For the filling, beat the cream until soft peaks form. Spread the cream over the meringue with a palette knife. Sprinkle the fruit and chocolate evenly over the cream. Use the paper to help you roll up the meringue from the short end. Once rolled, dust with the remaining sugar and cocoa. Ease the roulade, seam side down, onto a serving plate and refrigerate for 1 hour.

To serve, cut into slices and place, lying down, on a white plate to show off the colours.

The frangipane works with many types of fruit. In summer you can replace the pear with cherries, peaches, raspberries or figs, and in winter use poached quinces or prunes.

PEAR, ALMOND & MASCARPONE TART

SERVES 10

butter and flour, for greasing and coating
1 sheet good-quality sweet shortcrust
    pastry (bought or homemade),
    enough to line a 24 cm (9½ inch)
    flan (tart) tin (see page 195)
1 beurre bosc pear, lightly poached, then
    cut into quarters and core removed
65 g (2¼ oz/½ cup) toasted slivered
    almonds, to serve

ICING
125 ml (4 fl oz/½ cup) thin (pouring)
    cream, whipped
2 egg whites, whipped with 55 g (2 oz/
    ¼ cup) caster (superfine) sugar to
    firm glossy peaks
250 g (9 oz) mascarpone cheese

FRANGIPANE
125 g (4½ oz) unsalted butter, softened
125 g (4½ oz/1 cup) icing (confectioners')
    sugar
125 g (4½ oz/1¼ cups) almond meal
3 eggs, organic, if possible
35 g (1¼ oz/¼ cup) plain (all-purpose)
    flour

For the icing, gently fold the whipped cream and egg white through the mascarpone.

Lightly butter and flour a 24 cm (9½ inch) diameter loose-based fluted flan (tart) tin. Roll out the pastry until it is about 3 mm (⅛ inch) thick. Cut out a circle, allowing a 5 cm (2 inch) border around the base. Roll the pastry round over a rolling pin and gently ease it into the tin, pushing the sides in gently. Rest in the fridge for 30 minutes.

Preheat the oven to 180°C (350°/Gas 4).

Trim the excess pastry and prick the base a few times with a fork to prevent blistering and rising. Line the tart case with baking paper and uncooked rice and blind bake for 20–25 minutes. Remove from the oven, lift out the paper and rice. Return the pastry case to the oven and bake for a further 5–10 minutes or until the base has dried out.

For the frangipane filling, use electric beaters to beat the butter until light and creamy. Add the sugar and mix until well combined then add the almond meal and mix well. Add the eggs, one at a time, mixing well. Gently stir in the flour and mix well. Cover and refrigerate for 30 minutes.

Place the pear pieces neatly in the pastry shell and gently spoon over the frangipane. Bake for 35–40 minutes at 180°C (350°/Gas 4). Cool until just warm and remove from the tin. Allow to come to room temperature, top with the mascarpone icing and the toasted almonds.

I love this cake served served with honey yoghurt or a dollop of thick cream.

BLUEBERRY & LEMON CAKE

SERVES 8–12

350 g (12 oz) icing (confectioners')
    sugar
90 g (3¼ oz) self-raising flour
180 g (6 oz/1¾ cups) almond meal
finely grated zest (no pith) of 2 lemons
7 egg whites
185 g (6½ oz) unsalted butter, melted
1½ tablespoons milk
160 g (5¾ oz) frozen blueberries

Preheat the oven to 180°C (350°F/Gas 4).

Lightly grease a 22 cm (8½ inch) round cake tin. Line the base and side of the tin with a double thickness of baking paper to extend 2 cm (¾ inch) above the side of tin.

Sift the icing sugar and flour through a fine sieve into a bowl. Stir in the almond meal and lemon zest until well combined.

In another bowl lightly whisk the egg whites for a few seconds until broken down. Add the egg whites, melted butter, milk and 100 g (3½ oz) of the frozen blueberries to the almond mixture. Stir until just combined.

Spread the cake mixture into the prepared cake tin. Scatter with the remaining blueberries, gently pressing them into the mixture.

Bake for 1 hour and 10 minutes or until a skewer inserted into the centre of the cake comes out clean. (Be careful not to overcook the cake or it will be too dry.)

Turn the cake out onto a wire rack to cool.

This is wonderfully simple. To simplify it further, you could skip the crème anglaise and serve it with whipped cream or vanilla ice cream.

MEDITERRANEAN ORANGE CAKE WITH CARDAMOM CREME ANGLAISE

SERVES 8–10

180 g (6 oz/1¾ cup) almond meal
65 g (2¼ oz) fresh breadcrumbs
    (from day-old bread)
1 teaspoon baking powder
1 teaspoon finely grated orange zest
150 g (5½ oz/⅔ cup) caster (superfine)
    sugar
4 eggs, organic, if possible
160 ml (5¼ fl oz) vegetable oil

CARDAMOM CREME ANGLAISE
500 ml (17 fl oz/2 cups) milk
1 vanilla bean, split in half lengthways
    and seeds scraped
3 cardamom pods, bruised
5 egg yolks
70 g (2½ oz) caster (superfine) sugar

Preheat the oven to 170°C (325°F/Gas 3). Lightly grease a 22 cm (8½ inch) round cake tin and line the base and side with a double thickness of baking paper extending 2 cm (¾ inch) above the top of the tin.

Put the almond meal, breadcrumbs, baking powder and orange zest in a bowl and mix to combine. In another bowl, whisk the sugar and eggs using electric beaters until thick and pale. Gradually add the oil and beat until well combined. Use a large metal spoon to gently fold the dry ingredients into the egg mixture. Pour into the prepared tin. Bake for 40 minutes or until a skewer inserted into the centre comes out clean.

Allow to stand in the tin for 5 minutes before turning out on a wire rack to cool.

Meanwhile, for the anglaise, heat the milk in a saucepan over medium heat with the vanilla bean and seeds and the cardamom pods until almost boiling. Remove from the heat and discard the vanilla bean. In a large bowl, whisk the egg yolk and sugar and continue to whisk until combined. While whisking, pour the warm milk over the egg mixture. Return the mixture to the saucepan and stir over a very low heat until it thickens and coats the back of the spoon. Do not boil. Strain into a bowl to remove the cardamom pods and cool over a bowl of ice.

Serve slices of warm orange cake with a good drizzle of the anglaise.

If you'd like to glam up the cake, sprinkle the top with chocolate-covered roasted coffee beans. Or if you would prefer to skip the coffee, ice the cake with vanilla icing and fill it with strawberries and cream.

SIMPLE COFFEE & CREAM SPONGE CAKE

SERVES 8–10

butter, for greasing
190 g (6¾ oz) self-raising flour
50 g (1¾ oz) cornflour (cornstarch)
8 eggs, organic, if possible
2 egg whites
200 g (7 oz) caster (superfine) sugar, plus 4 tablespoons extra
2 teaspoons natural vanilla extract
½ teaspoon cream of tartar
whipped thin (pouring) cream, to serve
icing (confectioners') sugar, to dust

COFFEE ICING
185 g (6½ oz/1½ cups) icing (confectioners') sugar
80 ml (2½ fl oz/⅓ cup) strong espresso
20 g (¾ oz) butter, melted

Preheat the oven to 200°C (400°F/Gas 6). Butter two 22 cm (8½ inch) round cake tins and line the bases with baking paper. Sift the flour and cornflour together.

Separate 6 of the eggs then put all the egg whites together in a bowl (you will have 8 egg whites in total). In a separate bowl, combine the remaining 2 whole eggs, 6 egg yolks, 200 g (7 oz) plus 2 tablespoons of the caster sugar and the vanilla and use an electric mixer to whisk for 8 minutes or until the mixture is thick and fluffy.

Whisk the egg whites until frothy. Add the cream of tartar and continue to whisk to stiff-peak stage, gradually adding the remaining 2 tablespoons of caster sugar.

Fold one-third of the whites into the yolk mixture. Sift the dry ingredients over the top of the yolks, spread the remaining whites over the top and fold to combine.

Divide the mixture between the tins. Place the cakes in the oven, reduce the temperature to 170°C (325°F/Gas 3) and bake for 30 minutes or until a skewer inserted into the centre comes out clean. Allow the cakes to cool for 5 minutes, then transfer to wire racks to cool completely.

For the coffee icing, beat together the icing sugar, espresso and melted butter until smooth and creamy.

Spread the whipped cream on one cake and top with the other cake. Spread the coffee icing on top and dust with icing sugar.

The raspberry jelly is great but if you don't feel like the work, serve the compote with panna cotta or a favourite good-quality ice cream. Use any fruit you like in the compote – if it's stone fruit, be sure to skin and dice first.

RASPBERRY & CHAMPAGNE JELLY WITH SPICED BERRY COMPOTE

SERVES 6

200 g (7 oz) fresh whole raspberries
160 g (5¾ oz) caster (superfine) sugar
200 ml (7 fl oz) clear apple juice
6 x 4 g (⅛ oz) gelatine sheets
  (titanium strength)
250 ml (9 fl oz/1 cup) Champagne
  or sparkling wine
400 g (14 oz) frozen raspberries

SPICED BERRY COMPOTE
75 g (2½ oz/⅓ cup) caster (superfine)
  sugar
1 tablespoon clear apple juice
1 cinnamon stick
75 g (2½ oz/½ cup) fresh strawberries,
  hulled and halved
60 g (2¼ oz/½ cup) fresh raspberries
50 g (1¾ oz/⅓ cup) fresh blueberries
40 g (1½ oz/⅓ cup) fresh blackberries

For the jelly, combine the raspberries, sugar, apple juice and 160 ml (5¼ fl oz) water in a saucepan and stir over low heat until the sugar dissolves.

Bring to the boil, then simmer for 10 minutes or until the raspberries collapse and release their juices. Pour the mixture through a fine sieve into a bowl and let it stand for 10–15 minutes or until all the liquid has dripped through. Do not press down on the raspberries or the jelly will go cloudy. Discard the pulp.

Place half of the liquid in a saucepan and bring to a simmer. Meanwhile, soak the gelatine sheets in cold water for 2 minutes. Squeeze out the excess water, add the gelatine to the saucepan and stir until dissolved. Remove from the heat. Add the remaining raspberry liquid and the Champagne or sparkling wine, then allow to stand until the bubbles subside.

Divide half of the frozen raspberries among six martini or highball glasses. Pour over enough jelly mixture to just cover the raspberries, then allow the bubbles to subside. Refrigerate for about 30 minutes or until the mixture is set.

When the jelly is set, place the remainder of the frozen raspberries on top of the jelly and slowly pour over the remaining raspberry liquid, allowing the bubbles to subside. Refrigerate overnight until firm.

For the compote, combine the sugar, apple juice, 1 tablespoon water and the cinnamon stick in a saucepan and stir over low heat until the sugar dissolves. Increase the heat and simmer briefly until the liquid is a light syrup consistency but has not reduced too much. Add all the berries, simmer for 2 minutes, then remove from the heat. Cool, remove the cinnamon and place in a separate glass. To serve, spoon a little compote over the jelly.

This chocolate tart is inspired by Joël Robuchon's wonderful recipe. It is easy and has a wonderful taste and texture. It is simple: if you buy good-quality chocolate it will blow your mind; if you don't, it simply won't.

BITTERSWEET CHOCOLATE TART

SERVES 8–12

1 sheet good-quality sweet shortcrust pastry (bought or homemade), enough to line a 24 cm (9½ inch) flan (tart) tin (see page 195)
oil spray, for greasing
egg wash, for brushing
250 g (9 oz/1 cup) thick (double) cream
80 ml (2½ fl oz/⅓ cup) full-cream milk
200 g (7 oz) dark bittersweet chocolate, cut into small pieces
1 extra-large egg, whisked
cocoa powder (optional)

Preheat the oven to 180°C (350°/Gas 4). Spray a 24 cm (9½ inch) flan (tart) tin with oil spray.

Roll out the pastry on a lightly floured work surface until it is 2 cm (¾ inch) wider than the tart case. Roll the pastry over the rolling pin and gently ease it into the tart case, pushing the sides in gently. Rest in the fridge for 30 minutes.

Prick the base a few times with a fork to prevent blistering and rising. Line the tart case with baking paper and uncooked rice and blind bake for 20 minutes. Remove the paper and rice, brush the tart shell with the egg wash and bake for 10 minutes. Remove from the oven and increase the temperature to 200°C (400°F/Gas 6). Leave the tart shell to cool.

To make the filling, place the cream and milk in a saucepan. Stir and bring to the boil over medium heat. Remove the saucepan from the heat, add the chocolate and stir until the chocolate is completely melted and incorporated. Strain the egg into the warm chocolate mixture and stir until absorbed. Pour the warm filling into the cooked tart shell and smooth it with a spatula.

Turn off the oven and bake the tart for 20 minutes or until just set. Allow the tart to cool, then sprinkle with cocoa powder, if desired. (Do not refrigerate the tart.)

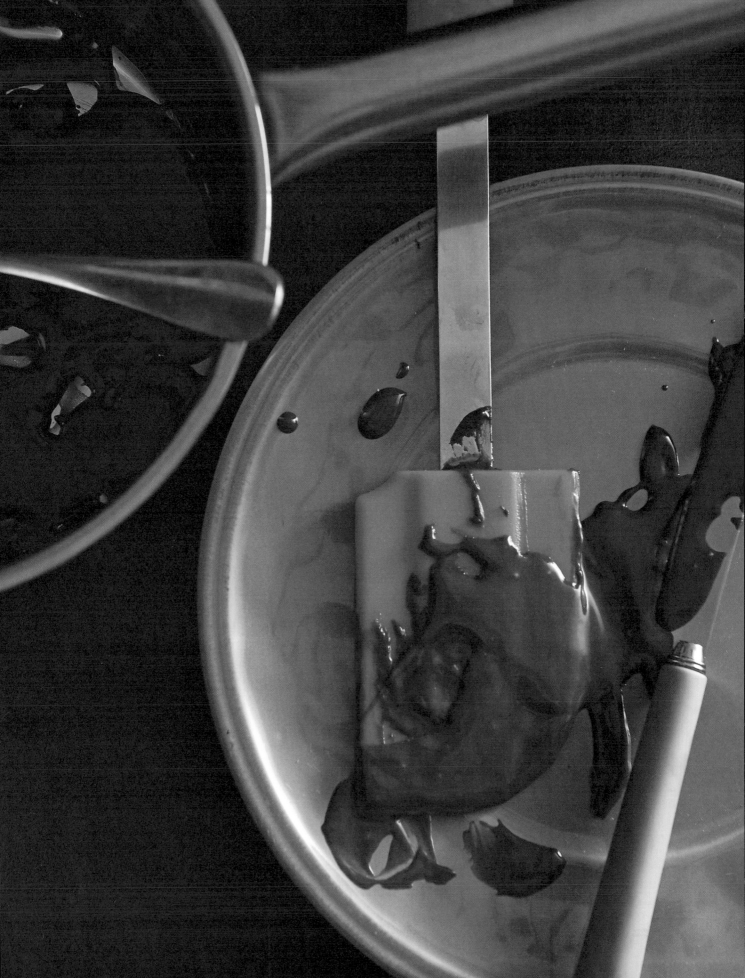

You can also try layering the tiramisu in individual coffee cups or classic martini glasses.

CLASSIC TIRAMISU

SERVES 12–16

300 g (10½ oz) caster (superfine) sugar
3 large egg whites
750 g (1 lb 10 oz) mascarpone cheese
200 ml (7 fl oz) espresso coffee
60 ml (2 fl oz/¼ cup) dark rum
250 ml (9 fl oz/1 cup) Marsala
24 savoiardi (lady fingers)
pinch of Dutch cocoa powder
20 g (¾ oz) good-quality dark chocolate,
    finely grated (see note)

Combine the sugar and 90 ml (3 fl oz) water in a small saucepan and stir over low heat until the sugar dissolves. Bring to the boil, then boil without stirring for 2–3 minutes or until the syrup reaches 112°C (234°F) on a sugar thermometer.

Whisk the egg whites in the bowl of an electric mixer until foamy, then with the motor running, gradually pour in the sugar syrup and whisk until the mixture is thick and glossy.

Use a hand whisk to whisk one-quarter of the egg whites into the mascarpone to loosen, then whisk in the remaining egg whites until combined.

Combine the coffee, rum and Marsala, then dip the biscuits in the mixture, turning to coat both sides.

Place a layer of biscuits over the base of a 24 cm (9½ inch) square (4 cm/1½ inch deep) cake tin. Spread with half the mascarpone mixture, sift over half the cocoa powder and scatter with half the grated chocolate. Top with another layer of dipped biscuits, the remaining mascarpone and scatter with the remaining sifted cocoa and grated chocolate. Cover and refrigerate for at least 6 hours or until firm.

To serve, use a large spoon to scoop out portions and place in serving bowls.

NOTE: Use a vegetable peeler to make long curls of chocolate to garnish.

Rum baba is a great dessert and is much simpler than it looks; make the cake, soak the cake, whip the cream and presto, fab dessert!

RUM BABAS WITH CREAM

MAKES 8

butter, for greasing

SYRUP
250 g (9 oz) sugar
zest of ½ an orange
zest of ½ a lemon
dash of natural vanilla extract
2 teaspoons good-quality rum

BABAS
3 g (⅒ oz) dried yeast
75 ml (2¼ fl oz) scalded milk, at room
  temperature
2 large eggs, organic, if possible
190 g (6¾ oz) plain (all-purpose) flour
55 g (2 oz) unsalted butter
1 teaspoon (superfine) caster (superfine)
  sugar

185 ml (6 fl oz/¾ cup) thin (pouring)
  cream, to serve
2 tablespoons icing (confectioners')
  sugar, to serve
good-quality dark rum, to serve

For the syrup, place all the ingredients and 500 ml (17 fl oz/2 cups) water in a saucepan and bring to the boil. Remove from the heat and set aside to cool.

Preheat the oven to 185°C (350°F/Gas 4). Lightly grease eight 200 ml (7 fl oz) ramekins with the butter.

For the babas, use a hand whisk to whisk the yeast and half the milk. In a separate bowl, whisk the eggs quickly, then whisk them into the yeast mixture. Add the flour and use an electric mixer fitted with a dough hook attachment to roughly bring the mixture together. On a medium–low speed, mix until smooth. Gradually add the remaining milk, mixing until smooth. Cream the butter and sugar together, then little by little, add the dough.

Place the ramekins on a baking tray. Fill each about half full with the mixture. Cover with a clean tea towel (dish towel) and leave in a warm place to double in size.

Bake the babas for about 25 minutes or until browned and evenly coloured. Remove from the ramekins.

Put the syrup in a bowl and soak the babas for 10 seconds while still warm to ensure they soak up a good amount of the syrup. Transfer the babas to a wire rack to cool.

Whisk the cream and icing sugar to soft peaks and set aside.

Just before serving, dip the babas into the syrup for a further 10 seconds then transfer back to the wire rack to drain a little. To serve, drizzle with the rum and serve with the syrup and a dollop of cream.

Panna cotta is the perfect finish to a flavourful lunch. If you want to be grown-up about it, drizzle the pineapple with good-quality dark rum – you'll be on your way to a pina colada.

COCONUT PANNA COTTA WITH PINEAPPLE

SERVES 4

125 ml (4 fl oz/½ cup) coconut cream (I like Kara brand)

250 ml (9 fl oz/1 cup) thin (pouring) cream

2 tablespoons caster (superfine) sugar

1 x 4 g (⅛ oz) gelatine sheet (titanium strength)

125 g (4 oz/½ cup) thick (double) cream

1 small pineapple, peeled, cored and finely chopped

2 tablespoons desiccated coconut, toasted until golden

Put the coconut cream, thin (pouring) cream and half the sugar in a saucepan over medium heat. Bring to the boil, stirring, then gently simmer for 1 minute. Soak the gelatine in cold water until soft, then squeeze out the excess water. Remove the pan from the heat and stir in the remaining sugar and the gelatine until both dissolve.

Strain the mixture into a bowl and chill over ice. It will start to set around the edges so keep stirring as it chills, making sure you scrape the bottom of the bowl. When the mixture reaches a gelatinous appearance (similar to the thickness of thick cream), remove the bowl from the ice.

Stir some mixture into the thick (double) cream to break it down, and then add back into the remaining mixture. Strain again and pour into four 125 ml (4 fl oz/½ cup) plastic ramekins. Place in the fridge for 2 hours or until set.

To serve, release the panna cotta by dipping each ramekin halfway down into a bowl of hot water for about 10 seconds. Gently place a small knife down the inside of each ramekin to create an air pocket and tip out the panna cottas. Serve the pineapple and coconut on the side.

You'll need to begin this recipe a day ahead, but it's worth it. Try garnishing with in-season berries for a delicious finish.

BAKED CUSTARDS WITH SALTED CARAMEL

SERVES 4

400 ml (14 fl oz) milk
175 g (6 oz) caster (superfine) sugar
1 tablespoon finely grated orange zest, no pith
1 cinnamon stick
½ teaspoon sea salt
3 eggs, organic, if possible
2 extra egg yolks

Place the milk, 75 g (2½ oz) of the sugar, the orange zest and cinnamon stick in a saucepan over low heat. Bring to the boil slowly, stirring occasionally. Remove from the heat and leave to stand for 30 minutes to infuse.

Meanwhile, for the caramel, place the remaining sugar, the salt and 100 ml (3½ fl oz) water in a heavy-based saucepan over medium heat, stirring gently, until bubbles appear. Stop stirring and continue to cook, watching carefully as the water evaporates and the liquid turns toffee coloured.

Carefully divide the caramel among four 125 ml (4 fl oz/½ cup) ovenproof ramekins, swirling to coat the sides and base.

Preheat the oven to 170°C (325°F/Gas 3).

Beat the eggs and extra yolks in a bowl. Slowly add the infused milk, stirring constantly, until well combined. Strain the mixture through a fine sieve into the toffee-lined ramekins. Place in a deep baking dish and add enough hot water to come halfway up the sides of the ramekins. Bake for 25 minutes or until a knife inserted into the centre of one comes out clean.

Remove the ramekins from the oven and allow to cool. Cover and refrigerate overnight.

To serve, dip each ramekin into a bowl of hot water to melt the caramel and run a knife around the edge. Invert onto a serving plate, allowing the caramel to flow down the sides. Repeat with the remaining baked custards. Serve immediately.

You can use any shaped ramekins for this recipe, or even tumblers or scotch or martini glasses.

CHERRY & YOGHURT PANNA COTTA WITH HONEYCOMB

SERVES 4

2 x 4 g (⅛ oz) gelatine sheets (titanium strength)
500 ml (17 fl oz/2 cups) thin (pouring) cream
1 vanilla bean, split in half lengthways and seeds scraped
50 g (1¾ oz) caster (superfine) sugar
150 g (5½ oz) Greek-style yoghurt
100 g (3½ oz) plain honeycomb, crumbled, to serve

CHERRY GLAZE
125 g (4½ oz) fresh cherries, pitted
25 g (1 oz) caster (superfine) sugar
1 x 4 g (⅛ oz) gelatine sheet (titanium strength)

For the panna cotta, soak 2 gelatine sheets in cold water until soft. Place the cream, vanilla bean and seeds and sugar in a saucepan over low heat and stir until simmering and the sugar dissolves.

Squeeze out the excess water from the gelatine and stir the gelatine into the cream mixture until it dissolves.

Place the yoghurt in a bowl, add half the warm cream mixture and stir until combined. Stir through the remaining cream mix. Divide the mixture evenly among four 125 ml (4 fl oz/½ cup) ramekins, cover and place in the fridge until set.

For the glaze, place the cherries, sugar and 250 ml (9 fl oz/1 cup) water in a small saucepan over low heat and stir until the sugar dissolves. Bring to a simmer and cook for 10 minutes or until the cherries are soft. Squash the cherries with a fork to release their juices then strain.

Soak the gelatine in cold water until soft. Squeeze out the excess water, add the gelatine to the strained cherry mixture and stir until completely dissolved. Allow the glaze to cool so it's at room temperature and just thickened. Gently pour the glaze onto each panna cotta then return to the fridge to set.

Serve with the crumbled honeycomb.

For a different flavour, replace half the cream with mascarpone cheese, mixing gently to combine. You could also swap the strawberries with whatever fruit you like.

STRAWBERRIES & CREAM WITH VANILLA SHORTBREAD

SERVES 4, WITH EXTRA SHORTBREAD

oil, for greasing

350 g (12 oz) hulled ripe strawberries, washed, dried and halved (or quartered if large)

160 g (5¾ oz) thick (double) cream

VANILLA SHORTBREAD

250 g (9 oz) unsalted butter, chopped

1 vanilla bean, split in half lengthways and seeds scraped

75 g (2½ oz/⅓ cup) caster (superfine) sugar

335 g (11¾ oz/2¼ cups) plain (all-purpose) flour, sifted

45 g (1½ oz/¼ cup) rice flour, sifted

Preheat the oven to 150°C (300°F/Gas 2).

For the shortbread, beat the butter, vanilla seeds and sugar in a small bowl using electric beaters until smooth. Stir in the sifted flours and press the mixture together to form a firm dough.

Knead the dough gently on a lightly floured work surface until smooth. (Do not overknead.) Divide the dough in half.

Roll out both halves of the dough to 23 cm (9 inch) rounds. Cut each round into 12 wedges.

Place the wedges on lightly greased baking trays about 3 cm (1¼ inches) apart. Bake for 25 minutes or until a light sandy colour. Leave to stand on the trays for 2 minutes before transferring to a wire rack to cool.

To serve, divide the strawberries among serving dishes. Top with a generous dollop of cream and serve with the shortbread.

NOTE: You can also serve these in martini or stemless wine glasses. You could also macerate the strawberries for 30 minutes with a splash of Cointreau or kirsch and then layer with the cream and crumbled shortbread.

Parfait is so easy to make and doesn't require an ice-cream maker – which is a big advantage. The salsa can be made from any seasonal fruit, particularly stone fruit and berries. You'll need to begin this recipe a day or two ahead.

LEMONGRASS PARFAIT WITH PINEAPPLE SALSA

SERVES 6–8

1 vanilla bean, split in half lengthways and seeds scraped

750 ml (26 fl oz/3 cups) thin (pouring) cream

3 teaspoons natural vanilla extract

5 lemongrass stems, pale part only, tough outer leaves removed, thinly sliced

330 g (11½ oz/1½ cups) caster (superfine) sugar

12 egg yolks

PINEAPPLE SALSA

400 g (14 oz) pineapple flesh, cut into 1 cm (½ inch) dice (1 small pineapple or ½ medium)

juice of 2 large oranges

small pinch of freshly ground white pepper

1 teaspoon pink peppercorns, lightly crushed

Place the vanilla seeds, cream, vanilla extract and lemongrass in a small saucepan. Bring to a simmer over medium heat, then remove from the heat, transfer to a bowl and when cool, cover with plastic wrap and refrigerate overnight.

The next day, combine the sugar and 270 ml (9½ fl oz) water in a small saucepan over low heat. Stir until the sugar dissolves, then increase the heat and cook until the syrup reaches 105°C (221°F) on a sugar thermometer.

Meanwhile, use electric beaters to whisk the egg yolks on medium speed. Pour the hot syrup slowly down the inside of the bowl, whisking constantly. Continue to whisk until cool.

Strain the solids out of the cream mixture and discard. Use electric beaters to whisk the cream to soft peaks. Once the egg yolk mixture is cool, fold in the cream. Pour into a loaf (bar) tin lined with plastic wrap and freeze for at least 6 hours (but preferably overnight).

For the salsa, heat a saucepan over high heat and add the pineapple. Sear the pineapple pieces for 1 minute or until they start to caramelise. Reduce the heat to medium, add the orange juice and white pepper, and cook for a few minutes or until the pineapple is tender. Remove from the heat and add the peppercorns.

To serve, dip the loaf tin into hot water for a few seconds, place a chopping board on top and flip over. Cut the parfait into thick slices with a hot knife, and place on serving plates. Top with a few spoonfuls of the salsa.

INDEX

PAGE NUMBERS IN *ITALICS* REFER TO PHOTOGRAPHS

First published in 2013 by Murdoch Books.
This edition published in 2017 by Murdoch Books, an imprint of Allen & Unwin.

Murdoch Books Australia
83 Alexander Street
Crows Nest NSW 2065
Phone: +61 (0) 2 8425 0100
Fax: +61 (0) 2 9906 2218
www.murdochbooks.com.au
info@murdochbooks.com.au

Murdoch Books UK
Ormond House
26–27 Boswell Street
London WC1N 3JZ
Phone: +44 (0) 20 8785 5995
murdochbooks.co.uk
info@murdochbooks.co.uk

For Corporate Orders & Custom Publishing, contact our
Business Development Team at salesenquiries@murdochbooks.com.au.

Publishing Director: Lou Johnson
Publisher: Diana Hill
Photographer: Earl Carter
Styling and direction: Sue Fairlie-Cuninghame
Design: Hugh Ford
Editors: Melissa Penn and Claire Grady
Home Economists on shoot: Sarah Swan and Mike Clift
Production Manager: Lou Playfair

The publisher and stylist would like to thank the following for their assistance during the shoot: Papaya for their generosity in allowing us to use their tableware; Georg Jensen Australia and Royal Doulton Australia for cutlery; and The Bay Tree Woollahra for tableware.

ISBN 978 1 76063 171 0 Australia
ISBN 978 1 76063 427 8 UK

A cataloguing-in-publication entry is available from the catalogue of the National Library of Australia at www.nla.gov.au.

A catalogue record for this book is available from the British Library.

Colour reproduction by Splitting Image, Clayton, Victoria.
Printed by C & C Offset Printing Co. Ltd., China

IMPORTANT: Those who might be at risk from the effects of salmonella poisoning (the elderly, pregnant women, young children and those suffering from immune deficiency diseases) should consult their doctor with any concerns about eating raw eggs.

OVEN GUIDE: You may find cooking times vary depending on the oven you are using. We have used a fan-forced oven in these recipes. As a general rule, set the temperature for a conventional oven 20°C (35°F) higher than indicated in the recipe.

MEASURES GUIDE: We have used 20 ml (4 teaspoon) tablespoon measures. If you are using a 15 ml (3 teaspoon) tablespoon add an extra teaspoon of the ingredient for each tablespoon specified.